THE
STORY OF
PINES

Bristlecone pines (*P. longaeva*) at an elevation of 10,000 feet, Death Valley National Monument, California. (*Dana K. Bailey*)

THE

STORY OF

PINES

Nicholas T. Mirov

and

Jean Hasbrouck

INDIANA UNIVERSITY PRESS

Bloomington / *London*

Library of Congress Cataloging in Publication Data
Mirov, Nicholas Tiho, 1893–
The story of pines.
Bibliography.
Includes index.
1. Pine. I. Hasbrouck, Jean. II. Title.
QK494.5.P66M57 1976 585'.2 74-30899
ISBN 0-253-35462-5 1 2 3 4 5 80 79 78 77 76

CONTENTS

PREFACE

WHY A BOOK ON PINES? Why single out a small group of about one hundred species for particular consideration? There are many reasons, but a most arresting one came to light not long ago: scientists announced their discovery that the earth's oldest known, higher living organism is a pine tree. It belongs to the species *Pinus longaeva*, commonly known as bristlecone.

For 4600 years this individual has lived high in the desert mountains of California, feeding, breathing, and reproducing its kind. In the same grove and in a few other groves are bristlecones that rival it in ancient age. To those of us who have worked with and loved pine trees most of our lives this is one more fascinating fact to add to the story of pines, but there are many other wonders that set the entire genus apart from other forest trees.

Throughout history man has shown a special affinity for pine trees. There are other useful conifers—spruce, Douglas fir, larch, hemlock—but none are as outstanding in importance as pines. Pines have affected man's religion, his dwellings, and his livelihood; they have inspired poets and painters, and have enriched the aesthetic aspects of human life in many other ways.

This book was conceived in the idea that nonscientific readers, on closer acquaintance with pines, might better enjoy and cherish these beautiful and fascinating trees. And while we address the nonacademic reader, we also can wish that a young student here and there may be inspired by the text to explore some of the unsolved biological mysteries of pines.

The Story of Pines is based on solid scientific facts carefully selected from a wealth of scattered material. Because pines have been valued as commercially superior trees, they have been studied widely by foresters, botanists, chemists, physiologists, and, lately, by geneticists. As far as possible, however, a textbook tone has been avoided here, for this story is written solely to share the authors' love for and appreciation of the world of pines.

For more than fifty years the senior author has observed and worked among these trees in many lands, from their north-ernmost appearance as the dwarf pine (*Pinus pumila*) in north-east Asia to the Merkus pine, the only species that crosses the equator naturally. In the laboratory he has experienced the joy of scientific discovery and the fascination of the unexplained. (What stimulates the germination hormones causing a pine embryo to grow? The trigger action is unknown.) He has found that there is a special enjoyment in that particular associ-ation with pines that goes beyond the domain of present-day knowledge into an area where both scientist and nonscientist stand wondering. It is a happy fact that to a nonscientist this area becomes more exciting in direct ratio to his increasing knowledge of pines and the challenge of the present limitations of science as applied to them. The senior author has demon-strated this to the nonscientist junior author with great success.

On a June morning after a rain we can walk through an incense-fragrant pine forest and realize that, if viewed as com-ponents of an ecosystem, most parts of the whole are elemen-tary and well known. It is possible to measure how much of the total rainfall was retained by the pine canopy, how much evaporated into the air, and how much percolated into the soil. Scientists can estimate how much water is used by the ecosystem and how much leaves it as run-off down the slope. All these processes have been studied and are known.

But how shall we analyze the effect that a cool morning and the pine forest have on scientist and nonscientist alike? They, too, have become a part of the ecosystem. How can the joyous feelings and wonder derived from pine fragrance, soughing breezes, and sprouting seedlings be pressed into a mathematical equation ($\Sigma = $ so and so)? That equation would be of such proportions that neither the labyrinthine computer nor the superprogrammer who could operate it exists today.

We expect some criticism for our use of personification in parts of the text. About this we make no apology. Our story tells of living beings whose life processes are often basically the same as ours.

So this is what our book is generally about—the relation of pines to man. However, with a respectful bow to the times, let us emphatically clarify our position by repeating that lovely old sentiment: "Our concept of man embraces woman."

NICHOLAS T. MIROV
JEAN HASBROUCK

ACKNOWLEDGMENTS

THE AUTHORS are especially grateful to Dr. John W. Duffield, professor of forestry at the University of North Carolina at Raleigh, for his helpful advice. We are deeply indebted to Dr. Dana K. Bailey for the quality of both his photographs and his encouragement, and to Miss Anne Avakian, former librarian of the U.S. Forest Service, for her invaluable research into pine history and mythology. To our friends at the Pacific Southwest Forest and Range Experiment Station, and especially to those at the Institute of Forest Genetics in Placerville, California, we wish to express our sincere thanks for their willing help. Grateful acknowledgment is given to the following: *The Atlantic Monthly* for permission to reprint "The Fragrance of Pines"; Macmillan Publishing Company, Inc., for permission to reprint excerpts from *The Golden Bough* by Sir James G. Frazer and from *The Evil Eye* by Frederick Elworthy; and to the U.S. Forest Service for permission to reprint parts of *A Tree is a Living Thing* from the U.S. Department of Agriculture Yearbook (1949). Our deep appreciation for photographs goes to the U.S. Forest Service; the Arnold Arboretum, Harvard University, Cambridge; the Philippine Forest Service; the New Zealand Forest Service; and the Australian Forest Service. And to our other friends who provided excellent photos, we are most grateful.

THE
STORY OF
PINES

I

The Pine Tree

*

Birth

F ROM A SEED that ripens in the autumn and falls to the
ground, a pine tree is born. Most pine species have winged
seeds that are dispersed by the wind, but some pines have heavy
seeds, the wings of which are short or rudimentary, or even
entirely absent. Wingless seeds cannot be carried too far by
the wind unless by a hurricane; they drop to the ground near
the mother tree and stay there, or they are dispersed locally by
birds and rodents.

Pick up a pine seed; crack it open. Inside the hard shell,
swaddled in a brown, leathery membrane, lies the kernel, commonly called the endosperm. It is palatable and sweet because
it is packed with starch, proteins, fats, and just a sprinkling
of sugars. Inside the kernel is cradled an ivory-colored rod, the
embryo pine. On one end of its tiny stem is a tuft of tightly
closed, pale leaves, or cotyledons; the tapering opposite end
will develop into the root.

Through the rainy autumn and over the cold winter, the
pine seed lies dormant under the forest litter of leaves and the
snow. In the spring, when the snow is gone and the dark, moist
soil warms up, deep changes begin to take place in the seed
already conditioned by the cold. The embryo pine awakens
from its slumber. What triggers its awakening? The cause is

3

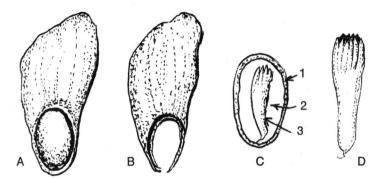

The anatomy of a Coulter pine (*Pinus coulteri*) seed. *A*. Seed as it comes from the pine cone, wing attached. *B*. Detached membranous wing. *C*. The split seed showing (1) hard shell, (2) endosperm or kernel, and (3) embryo. *D*. Embryo already displays tufts of seed leaves, but roots will develop later at the opposite end.

not exactly known, but what is known is complicated, indeed. Germination hormones are activated; the enzymes, whose function is to direct and hasten life processes in living organisms, begin to work on all fronts. Just as a bird's egg contains everything to nourish the earliest development of a new life, so does a pine seed. Sugars are used first; then starch is converted by enzymes, first into malt sugar and then into simple sugar—glucose, sometimes called dextrose. The proteins are split by their own enzymes into some twenty soluble amino acids, carriers of precious nitrogen. Seed fats (vegetable oils) are decomposed by an enzyme (lipase) into glycerin and fatty, mostly unsaturated acids. Glycerin disappears in general metabolism. Eventually fats also are converted into glucose and are used for the same ends as starch, although some unsaturated fatty acids serve other purposes (for making up lecithin, for instance).

Sugars, amino acids, and many minor substances rush to the embryo, where still other enzymes rearrange the amino acids into appropriate proteins, and where glucose is used partly for building the body of the plantlet and partly for oxidation (that is, slow burning) to provide energy for its growth.

The embryo develops rapidly. Soon the seed shell becomes too tight and splits open. The new pine tree is born. Its shoot begins to grow straight toward the sun and presently turns green. Often it wears, like a little brown hood, the remains of

These two handsome sugar pines (*Pinus lambertiana*) at the Institute of Forest Genetics, Placerville, California, were "incubator babies" grown not from seeds but from excised embryos, nurtured in test tubes, and then transplanted to the Institute's arboretum. In 1974, at age 34, the young pines look as normal as though propagated from the whole seeds. One is 70 feet tall and 26 inches in diameter. The other, somehow suppressed by her sister, is 67 feet tall and 24 inches in diameter. (*U.S. Forest Service Photo*)

the seed cover, the tips of seed leaves still in the exhausted endosperm.

So well has this embryonic stage of pine development been studied by scientists that foresters can actually produce "test tube baby" pine trees. The ripe pine seeds are split open, and the embryos are removed intact from the kernels and placed in test tubes where they are fed the same nutrients provided by the seed of the mother tree. The embryos develop, are planted, and grow into healthy, mature pine trees.

The root of a baby tree grows straight down in search of soil nutrients and water. Pine seeds prefer well-aerated, moist soil. They do not germinate well, if at all, in heavy duff, where bacteria release too much carbon dioxide. As soon as the root penetrates the ground, the seedling is permanently anchored, for better or worse, to the spot where it is destined to stay all its life. From now on, it will depend on the soil nutrients available in that particular place, and on the climate of that area.

In nature, fortunately, a pine seedling begins its life in the place where its ancestors have been growing for a long time, so the young tree is well adapted to the environment. But it also is exposed to local calamities, both physical (for instance, fire) and biological (insects or fungi). What happens to the pine later will depend not only on its environment but also on its heredity and its genetic capacities for survival amidst the continuous and relentless hazards of life.

When it emerges from the seed, the pine tree is as tender as a blade of grass. The green cotyledons (embryo leaves) free themselves from the shriveled endosperm and spread above the stem like the crown of a palm. In the first summer, a couple of weeks after germination, the baby leaves wither and are replaced by a tuft of primary (single) leaves. The secondary leaves—the pine needles—usually appear during the second summer (growing season), so that at the beginning of the third growing season the seedling looks like a little, full-fledged pine.

On the tip of the stem, tucked in between the seed leaves, is the terminal bud that develops into the trunk of the tree. The "leader" terminal bud is on top. The tree grows in height by annually extending its leader. If you were to drive a nail into the trunk of a pine—say at a point three or four feet above

Tip of a Scots pine *(Pinus sylvestris)* damaged by shoot-moth cater-pillars. They killed the leader (not seen in the photograph) and the first whorl of the buds, and mortally wounded all but one sprout of the second whorl. The survivor grew and is replacing the dead leader. The battle scar will remain for life. (*U.S. Forest Service Photo*)

ground—you would find the nail at the same height ten years later, although the tree's girth and height will have increased. (Foresters always measure girth at the same height—three or four feet above the ground.)

Branches spread more or less horizontally. Their tendency to grow vertically is inhibited by the hormones of the leading shoot. When the leader is broken by wind, damaged by insects, or clipped off by shears, the branches of the first whorl below the leader begin to grow vertically, and usually one of them becomes the leader.

The growing points of branches makes the pine's crown broad and spreading. In a healthy tree the growth points of the tip and the branches are active throughout its life. Roots also have their growing points, which are located near the tip of the root. Besides the growing points of stem, root, and their subsequent branches, another important growing region is soon established in the periphery, or cambium layer, of the stem. The cambium layer is an arrangement of cells, located between the inner bark and the sapwood, which makes the pine grow in girth.

About twelve to fourteen days after germination, a seedling begins lignification, or "making wood." That is the time when lignin first begins to accumulate in cells and makes a bond with cellulose to form the tough tissue of the tree. Before that day the little pine is almost pure cellulose.

Cellulose is a fibrous, soft material (cotton is about ninety-nine percent cellulose). It is the substance of lignin that gives the tree its mechanical strength. Whereas cellulose is chemically a simple straight-chain structure, lignin is complicated and so varying that some of its structures are not entirely understood.

In the pulp and paper industry, lignin is a problem. Cellulose is easily separated from wood by chemical methods, but a sludge of lignin is the by-product. Formerly lignin was drained off to pollute rivers and lakes, but today much of it is burned to produce energy. Other actual or potential uses are in petroleum drilling operations, in the reinforcing of rubber, in the preparation of plastics, as a component of glue, and in the production of vanillin that gives flavor to vanilla ice cream. Much research has been done on lignin, but more is needed.

We have touched only briefly on the complexity of a pine tree. In addition to cellulose and lignin, the major components are hemicellulose, waxes, simple sugars, fats, tannins, and other compounds. But lignin is the miraculous substance. Strengthened by it, the baby pine may grow from grass-blade size to a plant two hundred feet tall.

THE FRAGRANCE OF PINES

WHEN FOR the first time you contemplate a pine tree—tall and stately or stunted and crooked—you notice its fragrance. You inhale that fragrance when you walk through a pine forest or sit around a campfire made of pitchy pine logs. Perhaps you wonder why pines smell so good. They do not possess bright flowers; they are not frequented by bees and butterflies.

Pines do not need an alluring aroma to attract insects and assure their pollination. Their pollen is discharged from small, inconspicuous catkins. Gentle breezes carry golden clouds of pollen grains from one pine tree to another, to those destined to produce seeds. The Belgian poet Maeterlinck once called grains of pollen "those kisses of distant and unknown lovers." Foresters call those distant trees pollen parents.

The fragrance of pines is primeval. Compared to flowering plants, pines stand low on the scale of evolution. When pines originated, fragrance had not yet developed to that exuberant degree which we find in flowers—in lilacs, in violets, or in mignonettes. The aroma of flowering plants is a complex blend of alcohols, esters, aldehydes, ketones, and many other oxygen-containing compounds. The fragrance of pines comes from much simpler molecules of hydrocarbons called terpenes, with a mere sprinkling of oxygenated, more odoriferous derivatives. The difference between the fragrance of flowers and that of pines is about the same as the difference between a water color painting and a wood engraving: in one the desired effect is achieved by using a palette of many colors; in the other the effect is evoked by using only black and white. The fragrance of pine trees comes both from their bristly emerald crowns and from their predominantly brown trunks.

The fragrance of pine foliage is derived from essential oils emanating from the small breathing pores of the needles. The hotter the weather, the more essential oil is discharged to the atmosphere, sometimes causing a blue haze over pine forests. The composition of pine needle essential oil is very simple. It consists mostly of a pine terpene, appropriately called pinene, to which sometimes is admixed another terpene (limonene, a common ingredient of citrus rind essential oil, but it smells different), and a dash of a terpene alcohol (borneol) and a couple of its esters. The result of this blend is a delicate and ephemeral piney fragrance.

The evanescent nature of pine needle oil is caused by its volatility. If you put a drop of pine essence on your handkerchief, the oil disappears almost at once without leaving a trace of scent. It lacks what perfume manufacturers call fixatives, those substances like ambergris which hold essential oil and release it gradually.

Pine trunks also exhale essential oil, but in addition they exude resin. A minute injury to a tree, a tiny hole bored by a barkbeetle, a small wound made by a woodpecker, a windbroken branch—all these unavoidable adversities cause resin to ooze from pine trees. Sometimes, perhaps too much pressure inside the tree's resin passages may force droplets of resin to the surface of branches, cones, and even the trunk itself. These little pendants of resin hang on the tree, refract sunlight and break it into rainbows of color, and give off a piney fragrance.

Resin, as it comes from pine trees, consists of three kinds of substances: volatile oil, commonly called turpentine; the nonvolatile part called rosin; and the high-boiling ingredients, which not only hold back the volatile oils, causing them to be more lasting, but also, as perfume fixatives, have an unexplained and almost mysterious power to bring forth the full fragrance of the volatile ingredients and to soften their harshness. The natural fixatives also give off a faint and pleasant fragrance— just as the fixatives of the perfume industry. They become more volatile as the outside temperature rises. When pitchy pine wood is burned, not only the volatile oils but also the fixatives evaporate completely, and the rosin itself begins to sizzle and burn and decompose, giving off its fragrance. The Mayan Indians of

Guatemala still burn pine rosin as an incense in religious rituals.

Volatile oil composition is different in each of the one hundred existing pine species. In some it is very simple, consisting of the two most common terpenes, alpha and beta pinenes, which are found in many plants. It is sold in stores as paint thinner under the name of turpentine and is a product of the Landes region of France and of the piney woods of the southeastern United States. Often, however, volatile oil of pine resin is so unusual in its composition that it can hardly be called turpentine. Volatile oil of lodgepole pine growing in the Rocky Mountains is almost pure phellandrene, a turpentine of the parsley family of plants; its fragrance is grassy. Italian stone pine and some American pines possess a strange and unexpected fragrance, the volatile part of the resin consisting almost entirely of limonene. The fixative part of this Italian pine is a sesquiterpene called beta-caryophyllene, which occurs also in one desert pine of northeastern Mexico. The fragrance of the magnificent ponderosa pine of the western United States is determined by an abundance of an unusually sweet-smelling terpene with a charming name—carene.

In the Sierra Nevada of California grow two pines: Digger pine of the dry, hot foothills; and Jeffrey pine of the cool, higher altitudes. Volatile oils of their resin have not a drop of terpenes; their fragrance comes from several aldehydes much diluted with a gasoline-like substance called heptane. Heptane alone possesses no more fragrance than cigarette lighter fluid; with the addition of aldehydes it becomes pleasantly fragrant and fills the whole forest with a mellow odor described by some as vanilla and by others as pineapple.

Far above the Jeffrey pine forests, where patches of alpine meadows are studded with huge granite boulders, grows the undersized whitebark pine (*Pinus albicaulis*). Its exquisite scent comes from its resin, which contains terpinyl acetate, a common product of the perfume trade. Mellowed by an unusually high amount of gently fragrant sesquiterpene fixative and tempered even more by a bit of diterpene, the volatile oil of whitebark pine gives forth a fragrance not found in other pine communities.

On the arid Colorado plateau of the Navajo country grows

a pine known as the pinyon, or, by its Spanish name, *piñon* (*Pinus edulis*). Pinyons are very fragrant, and their sweet scent is largely determined by small quantities of a chemical called ethyl caprylate. (Strangely enough, this compound is also found in the higher boiling fractions of Zinfandel grape brandy.) Carefully blending ethyl caprylate with other fragrant substances, nature created a bouquet not found in any pine forests except those composed of Colorado pinyons.

Carene-bearing ponderosa pine often grows alongside aldehyde-fragrant Jeffrey pine. Some other pines with their own specific fragrances may be intermingled with these two. The blended fragrance of several species of pines becomes so complicated that it cannot be adequately described.

Why is there fragrance in pine forests? It does not help pines to reproduce themselves; what then is its function? We do not know for sure. If we attempt to explain its purpose, our explanation would be no more than an anthropomorphic guess. Scientists may tell you that when a plant is under stress, when it is forced to shift from aerobic to the anaerobic type of respiration, then volatile oils and rosins are formed and are an inevitable byproduct, and their fragrance is just an attribute to the structure of their molecules. This might be true, but there is another function of fragrance in pines, perhaps not useful to the trees and certainly not intended by nature: to give soothing pleasure, what Goethe called *süsser Friede*—sweet peace to mankind.

THE WOOD

WOOD FORMED in the spring is made of large, thin-walled cells and is called, appropriately, "spring wood." Toward the end of the growing season, as cells become smaller and their walls become heavier, they form "summer wood." Together these growths form "annual rings" that appear in the cross section of a tree trunk as concentric bands, the pattern of which depends on the exigencies of environment. When food and water are abundant and the pine is young and vigorous, the rings are wide; when summer rainfall is scanty, the rings are narrow. Thus by its living processes the tree "writes" on its tree-ring calendar whatever environmental conditions prevailed during each year of its life.

In warm and humid tropical lowlands, where there are no definite seasons and where no summer activity alternates with winter rest, the growth of pines is continuous and growth rings are not easily discerned. When various pine species are transplanted from their northern home to warmer countries, their behavior changes; some retain their inherited capacity, more or less, to form annual rings, whereas others form only a semblance of rings caused by intermittent dry and rainy periods. In humid tropical lowlands, it is not possible to tell the age of pines exactly by counting blurred growth rings. In the temperate seasonal climate of the North, a prolonged drought followed by ample rains may form an extra ring in the same summer. The false annual ring is generally not so conspicuous as the real annual ring.

As early as the fifteenth century, Leonardo da Vinci attempted to tell the age of trees by counting rings. Also he anticipated modern climate studies when he sought to determine the nature of "past seasons" by the width of tree rings.[1] Today, dendrochronology, the science of tree-ring study, has developed to such an extent that a piece of ancient bristlecone pine found in the western United States may persuade archeologists to revise their concepts of European pre-history.[2]

In the early 1900s the technique of studying tree rings was perfected into a precise dating aid. By studying tree-ring patterns in a wide area and knowing when a tree was cut down, dendrochronologists could make an accurate calendar. Old wood beams or fragments could be matched with dated patterns of tree rings, and their age could be determined to the exact year. Archeologists at the sites of Indian ruins in the southwestern United States used dendrochronology brilliantly, and the technique continues to have its most impressive application in the field of archeology.

In 1949, radiocarbon (C^{14}) dating was introduced as an

1. W. S. Stallings, "Some Early Papers on Tree Rings," *Tree Ring Bulletin* 3 (1937): 27–29.
2. See C. Renfrew, *Before Civilization: The Radiocarbon Revolution and Pre-historic Europe* (New York: Alfred A. Knopf, 1973).

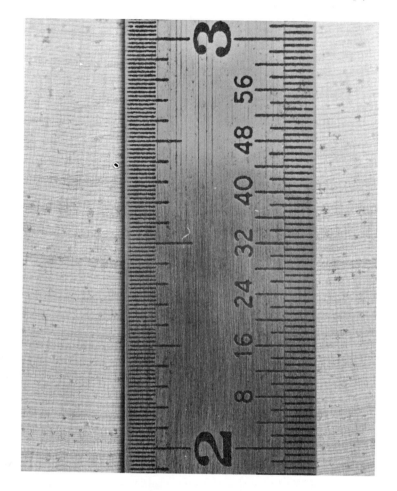

Cross section of bristlecone pine (*Pinus longaeva*) taken in 1948 from a dead trunk in the White Mountains of California at the altitude of 10,500 feet. It took 140 years to gain a one-inch increase of the radius. During some periods the tree grew better and the rings are wider (*top*). Dark dots are resin canals. (*U.S. Forest Service Photo*)

archeological tool. It was not as precise as dendrochronology, but it provided a tracer for age determination of almost all once-living things for the past forty thousand years. Radiocarbon, which is an isotope of the common element carbon, occurs naturally in growing things. In life it is absorbed, and after death it breaks down and is given off in "decay" at a measurable rate.

Tree-ring scientists were not swerved by the introduction of radiocarbon dating. They believed that their proven methods would be needed to verify general dating and to pinpoint the specific. And that has turned out to be exactly the case. Radiocarbon is formed in the upper atmosphere and scientists assumed that it entered our atmosphere at a constant rate. The C^{14} dating was based on that assumption. Now researchers have discovered that the assumption is not strictly correct, and that is where ancient pines (and, to some extent, sequoias) come in.[3]

Trees making annual rings anywhere in the world will have the same C^{14} content (within two years). That means that ancient bristlecone pines have been recording significant C^{14} data in their rings for several thousands of years. Wood from long-dead trees must be used for tree-ring study, and well-preserved specimens are available from the arid, high elevations of the White Mountains of California, home of the oldest bristlecones. By studying the C^{14} in bristlecones, researchers are correcting their radiocarbon dates. Already there is argument for drastic reconsideration of archeological history as workers consider artifacts in the light of the new dates. For instance, if the time scale is corrected to be eight hundred years older than previously thought, the Bronze Age and Iron Age cultures of southeastern Europe may have developed independently of the direct influence of Egypt and Mycenae.

Certain pines lend themselves well to the science of tree-ring study. Long-lived ponderosa, as well as bristlecone, is used extensively. A. E. Douglass, the acknowledged father of dendrochronology, preferred conifers for his early work in this field. His experiments began in 1901 and flourished at the still-busy Laboratory of Tree-Ring Research at the University of Arizona. Douglass took into account local false rings and also missing rings. He brought the mathematical and technical training of an astronomer to his testing methods. The exact planing of cross sections achieved precision in identification. The most sensitive ring record, he discovered, is made in dry or "stress" areas, where trees increase their girth slowly.

As J. L. Giddings, who did some early research in dendrochronology said: "The future of dendrochronology seems to be

3. Elizabeth K. Ralph and Henry N. Michael, "Twenty-five Years of Radiocarbon Dating," *American Scientist* 5 (September-October 1974): 553–59.

limited only by the enthusiasm of those who have the patience to learn its fascination."[4]

We are familiar with the appearance of the cross section of a dead tree trunk, but if it were possible to make a radial cut of a living pine we might better appreciate its anatomy. The living cells of the tree—in crown, trunk, and root—comprise only a small fraction of its entire bulk, perhaps as little as one percent.

Imagine a living mature tree, split in half-section from crown to ground. The trunk tapers because the younger growth is toward the top and has fewer growth rings; the oldest wood at the bottom of the trunk has increased its girth each year along with the newest wood. The silhouette of the tree's branches, or crown, tapers upward for the same reason, the oldest and heaviest branches being nearer the ground.

The outer bark of the trunk might measure four or more inches in thickness at the base. Just within the bark outline is the soft inner bark, or phloem, and within that is the light-colored sapwood, or xylem. The boundary between the active, moist phloem and the xylem areas is the all-important cambium layer, not visible to the naked eye.

In the tree's center is the widest column, the heartwood. Now it is nonfunctioning material, but it was sapwood in earlier years. It is dark because its dead cells are impregnated with phenols, including tannins, which resist decay. Also, the heartwood is heavy with resin (pitch). A ragged brown string of crushed parenchyma marks the center of the heartwood.

Where branches angle off the trunk, some strands of phloem and xylem simply bend outward from the main columns and become continuous with the growing branch. The same arrangement forms branchlets and twigs. Only the old branches have heartwood. Close inspection reveals that phloem and xylem tissue pass uninterruptedly in diminishing-size bundles through twigs and into the needles—the pine's leaves.

One needs a microscope to see the cells of the phloem and xylem and the life-giving cells of the remarkable cambium, the embryonic layer of cells that sheathes the tree from the ground

4. J. L. Giddings, "Development of Tree-Ring Dating as an Archeological Aid," in Theodore T. Kozlowski (ed.), *Tree Growth* (New York: The Ronald Press, 1962), p. 130.

to the ends of the smallest branches. Lying between the soft inner bark (phloem) and the sapwood (xylem), the cambium layer is only one cell thick. To the bark side the cambium cells produce phloem tissue which includes "sieve" tubes. Amino acids and sugars dissolved in water may pass through these tubes freely. These nutrients come from the chlorophyll cells in the needles and are dispersed for immediate use or storage. Toward the center of the tree the same cambium cells that produce the phloem also produce xylem tissue, including tracheids. A tracheid is a long, spindle-shaped cell filled with protoplasm when it comes from the cambium. After the cell has developed, the protoplasm soon dies and the tracheid becomes a water-conducting tissue only. In the growing season the prolific cambium makes myriads of cells, mostly tracheids, to form a new layer of sapwood. Pressed side by side, the tracheids lift water from the tree's roots and conduct it laterally through tiny pits on their sides—always in an upward movement. Enormous quantities of water and minerals are delivered this way, slowly but surely, to the crown of the pine.

The "mother" cambium layer is the continuously living part of the tree. During the warm part of the year, it never loses its capacity to give birth to both phloem and xylem cells throughout the life of the pine. In temperate climates, the cambium remains inactive in winter, resuming its work in spring.

Other cells to be viewed by microscope are the parenchyma cells, the little laboratories where nutrients, enzymes, and hormones are made. In the pine trunk they can be seen at work in the phloem and xylem. Parenchyma cells are fundamental plant tissue made up of soft cells such as the stem of the pine embryo or the chlorophyll-packed cells of the needles. The so-called rays, which extend radially from the center of the tree to the bark in bands, are made up of living parenchyma and dead ray cells arranged in one or several rows. In the center of the multicellular ray may be a horizontal resin canal.

Also under the microscope the system of resin ducts, discernible in the sapwood, forms a kind of broken-grid pattern, horizontal canals crossing vertical ones and extending through xylem, cambium, and phloem to disappear in the dense outer bark. Where resin ducts merge into heartwood their appearance

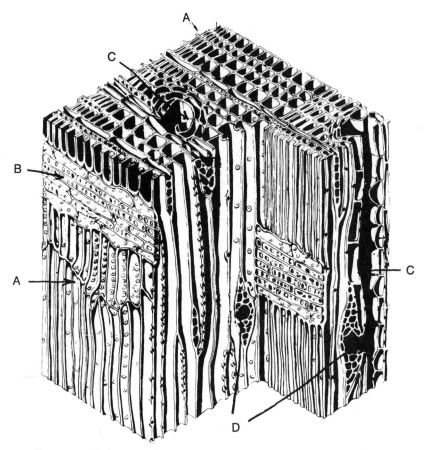

Structure of pine wood, showing different tissues. *A*. Tracheids, the cells which conduct water. Notice pits. *B*. Radial rays. *C*. Vertical resin canal. *D*. Horizontal resin canals; *right*, horizontal and vertical canals merge. (*U.S. Forest Service Photo*)

changes; they become clogged with pitch, just as all xylem cells have.

Resin canals are a telling feature in the anatomy of a pine. Of the multitudinous number of trees in the world, the abundant resin producers such as pine number only a few.

The Bark

In general, the outer bark characteristics of hard pine and those of soft pine are different, with, of course, some exceptions.

The bark of hard pines is rifted and coarse, more so at the lower part of the trunk, where it may form plates from four to six inches thick. The bark of soft pines is comparatively smooth, especially in young trees.

The fissured outer bark of a pine consists of dead layers of the inner bark. As cells proliferate outward from the actively dividing cambium to create new phloem tissues, the old cells are crushed against the outer bark with such pressure that random splits occur. Old phloem tissue newly exposed at the bottom of the fissures is no longer in contact with the supply of nourishment. It dries out, and the outer bark remains a hard protective covering over the vital parts of the tree.

The inner bark of soft pines remains alive longer than that of hard pines. As the tree's girth expands, the bark adjusts to growth, and less fissuring occurs.

Color as well as bark patterns vary with species; colors are predominantly brown, cinnamon, and dark gray. The comparatively smooth bark of young white pines is silvery gray, sometimes showing small balsam blisters which may have originated in the inner bark. (The chemical composition of such bark balsam is different from that of sapwood resin; thus it has a different fragrance.) Not all bark is drab. In Scots pine, and to some extent in closely related species, the bark in the upper part of the trunk is bright yellow, ochre, and orange—beautiful when late afternoon sunrays shine upon it.

The Needles

THE PINE tree's needles are its principal repositories for chlorophyll, the green-coloring material essential to photosynthesis. A brown or yellowed needle indicates that for some reason the fragile chlorophyll has disintegrated and the needle is not functioning. All healthy pines have green foliage. The gray-green of Digger pine is not a lack of chlorophyll but the result of a waxy bloom that covers each needle with a thin film.

As mentioned earlier, pine needles on a mature tree are its secondary leaves that have replaced the single, primary leaves in the first two years of life. Each needle develops from embryonic cells at its base. Issuing from minute, short shoots of the branches, needles grow in bundles. Their number per bundle varies in different species from one needle (in Nevada pinyon) to seven or eight (in Mexican Durango pine). But commonly needles are bundled in two's (jack pine, lodgepole pine, and others), in three's (most of North American hard pines), and in five's (as in almost all soft or white pines, one hard pine of

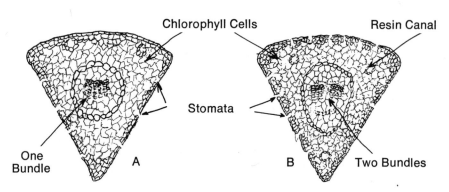

Difference in structure of soft (white) and hard pine needles. *A.* Cross section of whitebark pine (a white pine) needle. It has one water-conducting bundle of tissues in its center. *B.* Mexican (hard) Montezuma pine needle. Its water-conducting system is double. Both are five-needle pines.

Opposite:
A. Cross section of singleleaf pinyon pine (*Pinus monophylla*) needle, the only pine species having one needle per bundle. *B.* Cross section of needle bundle of Italian stone pine (*Pinus pinea*). Two-needle pines grow mostly in the Old World. *C.* Cross section of needle bundle of Jeffrey pine (*Pinus jeffreyi*). Most United States pines are three-needle species. *D.* Cross section of a rare four-needle pine bundle. Only two four-needle pines are known—the Parry pinyon (*Pinus quadrifolia*) of the southwestern United States and adjacent Mexico, and a Mexican white pine, *Pinus rzedowskii.* *E.* Cross section of a five-needle pine bundle. All but three white pines (pinyons excepted) have five needles. The only hard pines with five needles are found in Mexico, except the five-needle Torrey pine of California. *F.* Cross section of needle bundle of Mexican Durango pine (*Pinus durangensis*), the only pine which commonly has six needles per bundle, and sometimes seven or eight.

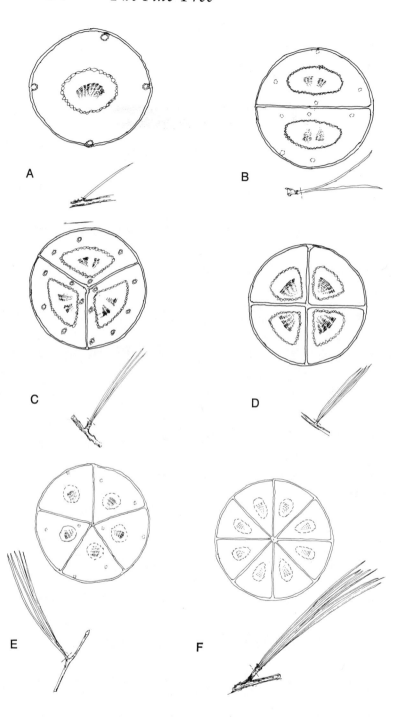

A

B

C

D

E

F

California, and several Mexican hard pines). A young tree in distress from fire, insect attacks, or even careless transplanting will revert to its infancy; it will develop the primary, one-needle foliage. Canary Island pine does this more readily than any other pine, and charmingly, because the primary foliage is a silvery blue-green.

From species to species needle length varies, ranging from less than one inch to about fifteen or even twenty inches. Needle length also may vary with individual trees in a species, depending on environmental stress. There appears to be a definite connection between climate and needle length, the shortest leaves occurring on alpine and boreal species and the longest leaves on species in or near the tropics.

In addition to bearing precious chlorophyll, a pine needle serves many good purposes for the tree. And it has a wonderfully intricate and efficient structure with which to do the job. Its skin (epidermis), which is waxy and waterproof, is provided with numerous openings (stomata) that have the capacity to open and close.[5] Through the stomata air is admitted to the inside of the needle and surplus water is evaporated into the atmosphere.

Each pine needle is the uppermost terminus of a strand of water coming without interruption from the tree roots, perhaps two hundred feet below. Water from the xylem of the branchlet enters the needle through central veins, or vascular bundles. Hard pines (diploxylon) have two vascular bundles in their needles, but soft pines (haploxylon) get along very well with one. These differing aspects of the needles help forest scientists to identify pines.[6]

Most of the space in the needle's interior is occupied by the large, irregularly shaped parenchyma (mesophyll) cells. It is in these specialized cells packed with green chlorophyll granules that the tree creates carbohydrate to sustain its life. Mesophyll cells surround the vascular bundles.

Among the mesophyll cells are found resin ducts accom-

5. "Stomata" is plural of *stoma*, meaning, in Greek, "mouth."
6. Haploxylon means a single fibrous duct; diploxylon means a double one. These logical names have been changed recently to *Strobus* and *Pinus*, respectively.

panied by thin-walled, resin-producing cells. Pine needle resin is a more fluid, more complex substance than wood resin. It is more volatile; when it emanates through the stomata it gives to the pine forest most of its specific, resinous fragrance.

The intriguing question of why pines are evergreen still awaits an answer. After all, pines are deciduous trees. They shed their needles, but they do it gradually—a little every fall—with the oldest needles going first. Needles may have a life of three, four, or even more years, varying with species and environment. In high altitudes needles may be retained for ten years or so.

THE ROOT

ABOUT TEN percent of the wood mass of a pine is in its root system. If not restrained by the environment, the total length of all roots of a mature pine tree may add up to many miles. In the forest, tree root systems intermingle to form a vast network underground, sometimes intergrafting with other pine roots.

A newly born seedling has a single taproot but soon begins to branch secondary roots. The principal parts of root growth are similar to that of stem growth, but the root has no cambium layer, no annual rings, and the relations between xylem and phloem are more complicated.

The root tip forms a rootcap, which shields the growing tip. As it pushes through bruising, rough soil, the rootcap may slough off cells and then renew them. When soil is deep, the seedling's taproot extends to a considerable depth; but if it meets a layer of hardpan, a rocky ledge, or permanently frozen ground, it develops a superficial root system. Generally, however, all pine species have a well-developed taproot.

In regions of rainless summers such as California, it is fascinating to follow the growth of a pine seedling when the soil begins to dry rapidly. The presence of moisture or lack of it is the difference between life and death. Generally at the depth of one yard there is enough moisture in the ground, unless it is depleted by surrounding pines. The taproot rushes downward to survive, racing with the receding moisture of the soil; when moisture is receding faster than the rate of the taproot growth, the seedling perishes. If a seedling's taproot can reach the depth where moisture is available through the first summer, it generally will survive.

A pine gradually develops two kinds of roots: sturdy ones that penetrate deeply into the ground and slender ones close to the surface. The sturdy roots, in addition to delivering water and minerals, anchor the tree securely. They also pick up any nitrogen that may have percolated deep into the soil. Although they branch and have feeding rootlets, the deep roots have no mycorrhiza (see below). The main function of the surface roots is to capture precious nitrogen from the forest's topsoil. In places where topsoil is always moist and amply covered with a layer of decaying leaves and humus, the surface roots are active throughout the summer; but in regions where summers are dry, the top layers of soil gradually become parched, and the shallow, slender feeding roots can function only in the spring. With the advent of summer they die, and new roots form when moisture is available again.

So far what we have described might also apply to many forest trees, but the root systems of pines are the focus of much attention among forest scientists because of a mysterious symbiotic relationship between the feeding roots of pines and fungi, which form a partnership to produce structures known as mycorrhizae. A few other trees and other plants have a similar relationship with fungi, but the symbiosis is well developed and perhaps the most studied as it occurs in pines.

Fungi are found throughout the world and have existed almost since life on earth began. Their species total about one hundred thousand, but only a few such as bread mold, mildew, and mushrooms are familiar to us by sight. All fungi are plants that have no chlorophyll. Like man and animals, they must have moisture and oxygen, and they must get their nourishment from organic materials. Fortunately, many species of fungi are busy helping to decompose and recycle the world's organic debris; otherwise the plants and animals that produced that debris would be smothered in it.

Where they grow in rich moist topsoil, many of the current year's feeding rootlets of a pine actually look diseased. Instead of being slender and tapering they are blunted, dis-

Mycorrhiza on a pine root. The happy coexistence of fungus and pine is beneficial to both. (*Visvaldis Slankis*)

torted, and minutely branched. Each root is encased in a gray-ish woolly sheath. A first look at the mycorrhizal state of the pine roots might suggest that this fungus, too, is bent on de-struction, but that is not the case. Something mutually bene-ficial is going on here.

The basic unit of fungus structure is a hypha, a small tubular filament which may be branched. A mass of these tangled hyphae forms a mycelium, the shaggy gray mantle that sur-rounds the infected root. The mycelium is generally a loose covering, from which threadlike tentacles extend inward to pierce the intercellular spaces of the succulent root. Oddly, the cells of the tissue apparently are unharmed. The mycorrhizal fungus is not a cellulose-eating one; it is a sugar-requiring one.

From the pine the fungus takes life-giving carbohydrates, particularly glucose, maltose, and sucrose. Some fungi cannot bear fruiting bodies unless associated with trees.

Scientists do not always agree on what pines take from this relationship, but it is acknowledged that pines cannot function normally in average soil unless helped by these fungi living in the soil. It is said that the friendly fungi may protect roots from harmful fungi, or that larger amounts of minerals are absorbed by mycorrhizal roots, or even that mycorrhizae may increase the drought resistance of pines. Some scientists emphasize the benefits of the increased absorbing area of mycorrhizal roots, and an exchange of growth hormones between the symbiotic partners.[7] The release of precious nitrogen also may be involved. As early as 1885 the German botanist Frank, who coined the name "mycorrhiza," registered his view that roots with their strange fungal sheaths constitute an independent organ of great importance to plant nutrition.

We know that Scots pine alone may form a partnership with any of more than forty fungal species, and a single fungus might choose among any of a large number of pine species with which to thrive. We know, too, that a pine can grow healthily without mycorrhiza if provided with proper nourishment, and that fungus was an established plant long before there were pines. Pine and fungus not only are unrelated but are widely separated on the plant kingdom's scale. Although much research has been done on the subject, the symbiosis of pine and fungus is still an intriguing wonder.

THE LIVING PROCESSES

THE ANCIENTS WERE RIGHT; a pine tree is inhabited by life. Its living processes are the same as in other higher plants, and some of these processes such as respiration and the digestion of fats are strikingly similar in both plants and animals. In their own way primitive people anticipated the tendency of today's

7. The interested reader is referred to J. L. Harley, *The Biology of Mycorrhiza* (London: Leonard Hill Ltd., 1959).

scientists to bridge the gulf between the animal and vegetable worlds. Those ancients who revered trees would not be surprised to learn what scientists know today—that the structure of a molecule of chlorophyll and a molecule of heme, the red pigment of blood, are almost identical. There are only slight differences, the most important being that the central atom of chlorophyll is magnesium, whereas the central atom of heme is iron.

Photosynthesis, which depends on chlorophyll, is operating in all green plants, but let us review it as it works for pines.

Photosynthesis

The most important life process in pines is photosynthesis, that is, building chemical compounds with the aid of light. The process is ongoing, but it is accomplished in two steps. The stage is set when water fills the veins of the needles and the surrounding chlorophyll-containing cells are moist. The stomata should be open, to admit air with its essential carbon dioxide, and there must be light. Step one: Light "excites" the chlorophyll in the mesophyll cells. With the light energy it "traps," chlorophyll splits the surrounding water molecules into separate hydrogen and oxygen. Step two: Air admitted through the stomata gives up its carbon dioxide to unite with hydrogen, and carbohydrate is made. Oxygen is released into the atmosphere. Note that only the first step of converting carbon dioxide into food requires light. Only about one percent of the solar energy falling on pine needles is used for photosynthesis.

Through the hundreds of stomata on the needle surfaces, air penetrates and gives about 10 percent of its precious carbon dioxide to the tree. The atmosphere contains minute amounts of carbon dioxide, only .03 percent by volume, or 3 parts in 10,000 parts of air. But the atmosphere is vast, and there is enough carbon dioxide to support the whole plant world.

The carbohydrate formed in the process of photosynthesis is glucose, the most common sugar found in plants, and the body of a pine tree is derived from glucose molecules. We are familiar with this form of sugar as honey, which is mostly glucose.

As pines are of northern origin, they thrive in temperate climates. Most favorable conditions for their photosynthesis are temperatures around 70° F and diffused, moderate light. Although pines are sun-enduring trees, on a hot and bright sunny day their photosynthesis declines.

Respiration

Opposite to photosynthesis, respiration is a living process in trees that consists of oxidizing, that is, burning at low temperature the same sugar—glucose—made by photosynthesis from nothing but carbon dioxide and water. The following equations show the energy flow in these two opposite processes:

Photosynthesis: carbon dioxide + water + energy of the sun expended ⟶ glucose + oxygen released.

Respiration: glucose + oxygen entrapped ⟶ carbon dioxide + water + energy released.

In daylight, when stomata are open, photosynthesis and respiration occur at the same time. Oxygen liberated in photosynthesis is used for respiration, while carbon dioxide released by the latter is used in photosynthesis. Most of carbon dioxide, however, is obtained from the atmosphere. Because normally photosynthesis is a more intensive process than is respiration, a surplus of energy is usually available for the tree in daylight. But when, under adverse conditions, daylight respiration becomes more intensive than the food-building photosynthesis, the pine finds itself short of glucose sufficient to keep it healthy. At night, when the light phase of photosynthesis is at a standstill, respiration still continues; glucose is oxidized and carbon dioxide is released, just as with humans. The tree uses part of the glucose made during the day. During the growing period, intense respiration is going on all the time in all living cells—in the needles, the roots, the sapwood, and the bark.

Whereas photosynthesis reaches its optimum on moderately warm days and decreases when the weather becomes too hot, respiration does not have such an optimum. The warmer it gets, the more intense is the respiration. Temperatures of 125°–130° F inside a tree are deadly. Respiration is less sensitive to the lack of water than is photosynthesis; thus during droughts, when photosynthesis stops, respiration continues and causes great harm to the tree. Even in dry, stored seed, respiration still goes on, but at a barely detectable rate.

During cold winter months in the northern pine forests, when temperatures may drop to −60° F or −70° F, respiration is practically at a standstill. The pine goes into a dormant period. Resumption of growth in the spring is—as the ancients observed it—like a resurrection of life.

Water Economy

All parts of a pine tree contain water, and all living processes take place in the presence of water. Mineral elements are carried upward through the wood from the soil in minute streams of water. The organic materials—sugars and amino acids—are transported by water through the inner bark from needles or from places of storage to bursting buds, to the ever-dividing cambium layer of the trunk, and (toward the end of the growing season) to the places of storage in the trunk and in the roots.

Water is absorbed by the roots, pushed into sapwood, and pulled up to the needles, a distance as high as two hundred feet or more in some pines. The water is then vaporized into the atmosphere through the stomata in a process called transpiration, the energy for which is supplied by the sun. About one-half of the solar energy falling on the pine crown is used for transpiration. Transpiration exerts a pull on the minute, continuous strands of water in the sapwood and causes water movement to the treetop. The incredible force that carries water to the tallest treetops has been a subject of intense study, and the generally accepted theory is that the transport of water is caused by the strong, cohesive force between water molecules in the sapwood strands.

The formation of 100 parts cellulose requires 55 parts water, but in this process nearly 1000 times more water than needed evaporates into the atmosphere in transpiration. Like all trees, pines are wasteful in their use of water. In one experiment in southern Germany, Scots pine was reported to take from the soil in summer about 2500 gallons of water per acre. But in comparison with other conifers, pines are conservative. In the same experiment European spruce lost in transpiration about 4000 gallons, and imported Douglas fir lost 5400 gallons per acre. Broadleaf trees, with their large foliage area, transpire even more.

Not much is known about how pines in arid lands adjust themselves to an unexpected abundance of water, but an example of such a situation occurred several years ago in California when a dam was built on the American River. In its lower course the river flows through dry hills covered with chapparal and with scattered Digger pines, a species that generally does not see a drop of rain for six or seven "summer" months. The dam caused flooding of the area. Now many Diggers find themselves growing so close to the water's edge that their roots are supplied with plenty of water throughout the dry season, but they do not look larger or healthier than other Diggers on the surrounding dry hills.

To prevent water loss during the hot hours of the day, pine needles have a hydraulic mechanism that permits them to shut off the stomata when transpiration is in excess of water intake by roots. But the very same stomata have to be open to admit carbon dioxide for photosynthesis. It is a dilemma for the tree: when the stomata are open the tree loses water, but when they are closed to save water the tree cannot assimilate carbon dioxide, that is, it cannot grow and function in a normal way. A balance between the two processes must be maintained somehow, and that is not easy to do.

In pines of the temperate region the stomata open their little shutters early in the morning; by noon they are beginning to close, and just before sunset they are almost totally shut for the night. During excessively hot and dry days the stomata open for only a short time in the early morning and then close for the hottest hours. As pines grow not only in the temperate zone but also as far north as the Arctic Circle and south to the equatorial region, undoubtedly the opening and closing of stomata under such different conditions vary considerably. At present we can say only that there is no overall regularity in the opening and closing of stomata in different pine species and in different environments.

Soil Nutrition

The food of a pine tree consists almost entirely of the most common elements: hydrogen, oxygen, and carbon, available from water or from air. The bulk of a pine tree is created from these three substances; the remainder is obtained chiefly from the soil. The ten major elements necessary for the growth and well-being of a pine tree are as follows: carbon (C); hydrogen (H); oxygen (O); nitrogen (N); phosphorus (P); potassium (K); calcium (Ca); magnesium (Mg); sulfur (S); iron (Fe).[8] They are needed in relatively large amounts, but the greatest demand is for nitrogen, potassium, and phosphorus. (The letters NKP on every fertilizer bag indicate those three elements.)

Of all the required elements, nitrogen stands apart. Animals, unless they are blood-suckers or carnivores, procure nitrogen directly from plants; but most plants, of course, have to depend on a number of supply sources, some of them uncertain. Every pine cell, every nucleus, and every pollen grain needs nitrogen, which promotes growth; without it, cells cannot divide. Nitrogen is an ingredient not only of all amino acids and proteins but also of some secondary substances found in pines such as alkaloids or some vitamins. A tree with enough nitrogen has healthy, green foliage, and its growth is luxuriant. If deprived of sufficient nitrogen, the pine's needles turn pale green.

Four-fifths of the air consists of nitrogen, but it is found there in inert form. Nature releases minute amounts of this ample supply through a series of conversions triggered by lightning during thunderstorms. But pines must depend also on recycled nitrogen from decaying vegetation or dead animals on

8. To assist his students in remembering the names of major elements needed for higher plants, one professor of botany taught the following cabalistic sentence that makes little sense but helped many in their exams: "See HOPK'NS Ca-Fe, Mighty good." "See" stands phonetically for C (carbon); H for hydrogen; O for oxygen; P for phosphorous; K for potassium (kalium); N for nitrogen; S for sulphur; Ca for calcium; Fe for iron (ferrum); and "Mighty good," with a certain laboriousness, stands for magnesium (Mg).

Results of a hydroponics experiment with ponderosa pine (*Pinus ponderosa*) seedlings all of the same age. Instead of in soil, the seedlings were grown in water and minerals, and show their response to different solutions. *Left to right:* Complete nutrient solution; minus calcium; minus magnesium; minus sulfur; minus potassium; minus phosphorus; minus nitrogen. The seedlings suffered the most when deprived of nitrogen, phosphorus, and potassium, in that order. Hydroponics is the term introduced by Dr. W. F. Gericke for the technique of growing plants in nutrient solution. (*U.S. Forest Service Photo*)

the ground. Nitrogen-fixing bacteria in the topsoil contribute, and, in some instances, shrubs and herbs equipped with nitrogen-fixing bacterial nodules on their roots may help. Mycorrhizal fungi may be of assistance in the ever-present striving for nitrogen.

Pines often grow in dry climates and on soils so poor that not much litter is formed for bacteria and fungi to thrive on. Normally wild pines have barely enough nitrogen to suffice. Early plantings of pine forests in the southern hemisphere (New Zealand and Java) utilized rich soil and pines grew luxuriously. But growing populations have changed conditions. Now pines generally are planted on soil too poor for agriculture.

In addition to the major elements, pines demand for their

well-being minute amounts of such unexpected trace elements as manganese, copper, boron, and zinc.

Growth

Through the process of photosynthesis, with an adequate supply of water and the help of nitrogen and mineral elements, both major and minor, a pine tree builds its body. In some pines, mostly those of California (sugar pine, ponderosa pine, Jeffrey pine), as much as two thousand cubic feet of organic matter, chiefly wood, may accumulate in each tree.

But the growth of a pine is not merely an accumulation of organic matter. Growth is an involved physiological process in which the use of building materials is regulated by environment, genetic programming, and growth hormones. Warmth, light, fertile soil, air, and moisture are needed. Withholding these essentials is the method used by the Japanese in dwarfing pines, some of which, grown in small pots, may be several hundred years old. Any pot-bound young pine is checked in its growth and is more or less dwarfed.

Temperature increase of about 18° F doubles the rate of chemical reactions in plants. When temperatures are too low or too high for a proper functioning of the organism, many disturbances occur and growth is retarded, although the tree may continue to live. The optimum temperature for the growth of a pine, that is, accumulation of wood, is not necessarily the same as the optimum temperature for its development.

Because pines are northern plants they developed in regions with alternating seasons—a warm one when they grow and a cold one when they rest. In a temperate climate, the annual shoot of a pine at the tip of each branch completes its growth early in the season, and toward midsummer a terminal bud is formed. By that time, all cell division for the next year's growth pattern is completed in the buds, and for the rest of the summer they remain dormant. This means that the next year's growth pattern is determined several months in advance: all microscopic needle-bundle shoots are set; all microscopic catkins and conelets are formed. The next summer's growth of all these parts is merely the elongation of the cells prefabricated last season. Growth in girth continues throughout the summer by division and expansion of the cambium cells.

A long time before cold weather arrives, the pine already has completed its seasonal growth. It then prepares itself for winter, shedding part of its needles but retaining its evergreen crown. It removes most of its water from the cells into the intercellular spaces, lest the expansion of freezing burst the cell and kill the protoplasm. The pine then goes into hibernation. It can withstand intense winter cold when temperatures in the forests of Siberia or in Montana drop to −60° F and even lower.

Unusually warm weather in late winter may cause a pine to resume growing and to open its buds; subsequent cold weather then will kill the new, tender shoots. That is why a northern pine might suffer from a spring frost when transplanted to the balmy south or when introduced into tropical lowlands, where the seasons are distorted and there is neither winter dormancy nor spring conditioning for their summer. Growth becomes continuous; branches are not formed, and the stem, which is extended abnormally, looks like a thin whip covered with needles. Eventually wind breaks it. This growth without proper development (caused by strange environment) is called "foxtailing" (*cola de Zorro* in Spanish) and causes foresters a great deal of trouble. The abnormality is found in Monterey pine growing in Hawaii, in slash pine growing in Argentina and Brazil, and occasionally in other pines introduced into the tropics.

It is important for many pine species that their seeds also go through a period of preparatory changes necessary for germination. This period is commonly called the after-ripening. When it is not fulfilled, the seeds do not germinate. In some species this period is short or even totally absent, and after-ripening is not needed there. In other species it extends for three months or even longer.

For normal growth of pines, light must be available in proper intensity and quality. When light is lacking, pines cannot make organic matter; they suffer and die. In deep shade, pines grow and develop differently than they do in full light. They are spindly and their crowns are narrow and unhealthy.

When mass production of pines from desirable trees is planned, foresters take advantage of a willingness that some

"Foxtailing" of Monterey pine (*Pinus radiata*) planted in Hawaii. The tree is 5 years old and its branchless part is 19½ feet long. The aberration is caused by uniformity of warm and humid climate. *Right background:* Almost all other pines are normal. (*R. M. Lanner*)

pines have to propagate vegetatively. It is possible to induce striking roots in cuttings and needle bundles, or to graft branchlets and buds of one pine species to another, but pines vary in their capacity to strike roots on cuttings. Monterey pine is the easiest (but not so easy as, for instance, willows) to propagate by cuttings; sugar pine is the most difficult. The best way to propagate sugar pine vegetatively is to use the ancient Chinese method of "air layering," that is, girdling a branch and applying to the wound a damp moss compress. Vegetative propagation is the most rapid method for mass reproduction from a desirable tree that has been chosen for its disease or insect resistance, attractive form, or exceptionally long fibers.

Resin Production

The origin of the legend of Pitys (see chapter 2) is easy to imagine; anyone can see that a pine tree weeps glistening tears. The "tears" are drops of oleoresin, commonly called resin, pitch, or even gum. When the trunk is slashed, the tears appear almost immediately if the day is warm. With resin a pine heals its wounds, and attracts and traps certain insects and kills them. Possibly resin has other functions in the life of trees, but we don't know about those yet.

Resin is a honey-like mixture of hard rosin and liquid turpentine.[9] As we described in the morphology of the tree, resin is produced by special cells surrounding the vertical and horizontal canals throughout the trunk of the pine. (Roots and needles also contain resin but in small amounts.) As pine is extremely sensitive to injury, any cut through to the inner bark begins a flow of resin to the wound. At the same time, the formation of new resin canals begins above and below the site of the injury, and the surrounding cells squeeze more resin into the canals. It is the remarkable ability of the pine to form additional resin canals after having been wounded that has made this system most valuable to both trees and mankind.

The turpentine industry is based on this emergency response of the pine. Carefully planned gashes in the "turpentine trees" draw resin, which is then gathered in containers attached to the trunk. Severe and frequent wounding would kill a pine tree, but reasonable tapping, or hacking, once or twice a week, is harmless. It is like milking a cow. It could be continued for several years and, at least theoretically, the total weight of the resin obtained might be more than the weight of the entire tree!

A few conifers related to pines have resin canal systems,

9. For an explanation of confusing naval stores terminology, see the glossary in N. T. Mirov, "Composition of Gum Turpentines of Pines," U.S. Forest Service Technical Bulletin No. 1239 (Washington, D.C.: Government Printing Office, 1961).

but those of pines are more efficient than those of any other tree. The importance of oleoresin to industry has made it the object of intensive study by foresters, who have discovered that different species of pines have different oleoresin chemistry. This same discovery supports the theory that the chemical evolution and the morphological evolution of pines have developed independently.[10]

Living cells of sapwood occasionally produce large amounts of various unusual substances. Sugar pine of the Pacific coast and *Pino de azucar* ("sugar") of Mexico (*Pinus ayacahuite*) yield much of a sugary substance often accumulating on fire scars, a cyclic sugar (methyl-inositol) that is sweet and purgative. Inositol is a kind of complicated alcohol found in plants. All pines have minute amounts of inositol in their cells, but the abnormally high concentration of one of its derivatives in the two white pines can be explained only by a chance chemical mutation serving no useful purpose that we know.

Such unexpected things happen in nature—occasionally much to the consternation of man. To illustrate, there is the case of the "gasoline tree" in the early days of the commercial turpentine industry in California:

At the beginning of the Civil War, when Union forces were cut off from their normal turpentine sources in the Southeast, turpentine production was started in the plentiful forests of the California foothills. All went well if resin was taken from the ponderosa pine, but what turpentiners didn't know was that ponderosa forests are replaced imperceptibly by Jeffrey pine, beginning at an elevation of about five thousand feet. (The two species look so much alike that even today experts have trouble telling them apart.) A pitch collector tapping a ponderosa gathered ordinary resin from which he would distill ordinary turpentine. But if he unwittingly tapped a Jeffrey pine, he gathered pitch containing heptane—the same highly inflammable heptane that is found in petroleum as it is pumped from oil wells. At that time no one knew about the Jeffrey's strange chemistry. Firing up a primitive turpentine still loaded with Jeffrey pitch

10. N. T. Mirov, "Composition of Turpentine of Lodgepole and Jack Pine Hybrids," *Canadian Journal of Botany* 34 (1956): 443–57.

was like building a fire under a gasoline tank. Heptane must be distilled very carefully.

Later, in 1890, a California druggist named D. F. Fryer distilled heptane in his laboratory and sold it under the name "Abietine" (oil of fir) as a remedy for pulmonary ailments and a cure for tuberculosis. Not until the early 1900s did chemists agree that Jeffrey "turpentine" is ninety-five percent "normal" heptane C_7H_{16}, the seventh member of the most primitive hydrocarbons group, methane series, now called alkanes. Digger pine also was proved to have a high percentage of heptane, and much later it was found to a lesser degree in some Mexican pines. Sir John Simonsen (the only turpentine man in history to be knighted), who worked with pines in India in the 1920s, ventured to suggest that the presence of alkanes in pine oleoresins perhaps indicates that ancient pines contributed to the formation of petroleum.

It was the destiny of the senior author to become involved in a later round involving Jeffrey pine heptane, the same primitive hydrocarbon in motor fuels that makes automobile engines "knock." In 1924, when the gasoline industry initiated tests that would result in smoother gasolines, a supply of heptane was needed for the research work. By chance, the author had a small supply available because he had been experimenting with Jeffrey oleoresin. Later he was in charge of field work for a project that provided the Ethyl Gasoline Corporation with pure pine heptane. Then, within two years, a less complicated method of testing motor fuels in the laboratory was discovered. Oleoresin from the "gasoline tree" was no longer in demand. But it was with the help of a pine tree that the late Dr. Graham Edgar, then director of research for the Ethyl Corporation, devised his now-famous "octane" scale for measuring the knocking qualities of motor fuels.

Today the strange chemistry of Jeffrey pine is important only as an historical curiosity.

Maturity and Reproduction

Different pine species reach sexual maturity at different ages. Often young pines, merely two or three years old, develop female conelets and male catkins, but this development should not be taken seriously; their reproductive precocity is only temporary, and usually they soon go back to vegetative life. A real reproductive stage comes when the pine is mature and strong, capable of producing seeds steadily.

Not only seed-bearing age but the intervals between seed years vary in different species. Seed bearing is a taxing ordeal for the mother tree. Because much material and much energy are needed for producing a crop of cones, good seed years don't happen every calendar year; they occur at two-, three-, and even five-year intervals. Vegetative growth of the mother tree dwindles during the seed years, and the annual rings of its trunk become conspicuously narrower than before. Periodicity of seed years in pines depends on a combination of nutrition, weather, and the genetics of the species.

Three centuries B.C. Theophrastus wrote that "opinions differ as to whether pines have true flowers, but definitely they have 'flowering tufts,' both male and female on the same tree." What he observed were the male and female conelets, or strobili. We have described how these organs were initiated at the end of the previous summer. They reach their full development in the spring of a flowering year.

The male "tuft," now commonly called catkin, is a small conelet in which tiny scales are arranged around an axis. On the underside of each scale develop two pollen sacs. In these spore sacs (microsporangia) of the catkins develop "pollen mother cells," which undergo chromosome reduction division, each pollen mother cell producing four microspores in which the twenty-four chromosomes of the parent tree are reduced by half. The microspores develop into pollen grains. At maturity pollen sacs are packed tight with ripe pollen grains, each of which is a sperm cell with twelve chromosomes instead of the twenty-four. Each pollen grain is equipped with two air sacs which make pollen buoyant and carry it over long distances even in a gentle breeze. So much pollen is dispersed that in the vicinity of pine forests it is everywhere; it becomes a sulfur-yellow scum on lakes, or dust on the table in your tent and on your books.

Almost all of these pollen grains perish; only a few reach

female "tufts" (commonly called conelets). Ideally the pollen reaches trees of its own species but not its parent tree. When self-pollination (foresters call it inbreeding) does happen, it results in weak progeny. If pollen lands on the conelet of another pine species, and if the two species are compatible, the union is consummated. A hybrid may be produced.

While pollen grains were being initiated and developed, complicated changes were taking place in the female conelet, which is much larger than the male conelet and of about the same structure. The female conelet has a central axis to which are attached leaves modified to scales. On the upper side of each scale develop two ovules, and in each ovule a mother cell is formed. This cell undergoes two divisions, during one of which (as in pollen) the number of chromosomes is reduced by half. So now both male parent and female parent are equally represented for a happy union.

When clouds of pollen fill the air and begin settling everywhere, the female conelets already are waiting to be fertilized.

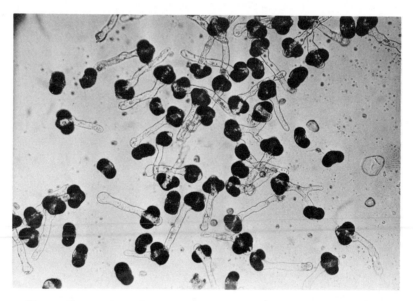

Pine pollen grains of spruce pine *(Pinus glabra)* in germination stage. Note transparent pollen tubes through which sperm is discharged when pollen reaches the female conelet. *(U.S. Forest Service Photo)*

Their tender scales are slightly separated. Between the scales appears a rarely observed sugary droplet, and, as soon as a pollen grain touches it, the surface tension is broken and the pollen grain is pulled inside the conelet. Once inside, the pollen comes into contact with the pearly mass of spongy tissue or nucellus. Immediately the pollen grain germinates, sending its "pollen tube" through the tender tissue.

During the first summer the pollen tube does not make much progress; it stops growing even before the cold weather sets in. It resumes its growth only the following spring, when it reaches the female reproductive structure, which already has undergone further changes.

The "mother cell" of the ovule is divided into egg cells numbering from two to six, with accompanying nutritive tissues. Cells of the whole structure have a haploid number (twelve) of chromosomes. When the pollen tube reaches an egg cell, one of the two pollen nuclei unites with the egg cell nucleus. As both have haploid numbers of chromosomes, the fertilization (union) results in a cell (zygote) with twenty-four chromosomes—as in the parent tree.

The fertilized egg undergoes more development and more changes, some of which appear to be necessary only for reminding the pine tree that its ancestors were ferns and mosses. Anatomically, one fertilized egg can produce forty-eight embryos, but in nature only one embryo (rarely two or three) develops into a pine tree; the remainder wither and die.

After fertilization the female conelet begins to grow fast. It reaches its full size at the end of the second summer, counting from pollination, and discharges its ripe seeds. There are, however, exceptions to the two-summer time of maturation: Mediterranean stone pine, Canary Island pine, Mexican Chihuahua pine, and possibly California Torrey pine need three growing seasons to develop a mature cone. In tropical regions—Central America, for instance—where there are no definite four seasons, the local pines, *Pinus teocote* or *Pinus oocarpa*, take less than two summers to produce cones and ripen seeds. How pines planted in the humid equatorial lowlands manage to produce cones, shed pollen, and mature seeds is still not well known.

There are exceptions, too, in the manner of discharging ripe

Female conelets (enlarged) of bristlecone pine (*Pinus longaeva*) already pollinated and growing. (*Dana K. Bailey*)

seeds. Most pines disseminate the seeds as soon as they are ripe, but some species, called closed-cone pines, like the knobcone pine prefer to keep their seeds inside the cones. Their cone scales are tightly cemented together. Only when the mother trees are scorched by fire do the cone scales open; the seeds fall upon the burned ground and the destroyed forest is regenerated. Closed-cone pines possess an amazing capacity to keep their seeds fresh and viable in their cones for many years. A case is known where a lodgepole pine cone was kept in a desk drawer for thirty years, yet its seeds still retained their viability.[11] These

11. Sugars, starch, and proteins are not so susceptible to deterioration in storage as are pine seed oils, which are almost all unsaturated and thus vulnerable to oxidation. Eventual loss of life in stored seeds is apparently caused by changed structure of chromosomes. The longer you store the seeds, the more freaks you may expect among the seedlings, which show that the inheritance mechanism has deteriorated.

Branch of a mature ponderosa pine showing, on the tip (*top*), three young conelets ready for fertilization; *center*, three mature cones containing seeds; *bottom*, two open cones from which seeds have fallen. (*U.S. Forest Service Photo*)

Pine cone size varies widely. *A*. Sugar pine cone, the largest cone. *B* and *C*. Colorado pinyon (*Pinus edulis*) and lodgepole (*Pinus contorta*) cones, two of the smallest. *D*. Coulter pine cone, one of the heaviest.

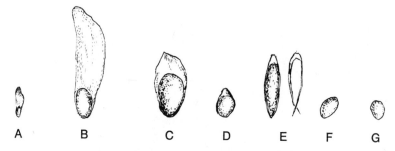

Various pine seeds, reduced size. *A.* Mexican weeping pine. *B.* Long-leaf pine. *C.* Digger pine. *D.* Limber pine. *E.* Chilghoza pine. *F.* Pinyon pine (wingless). *G.* Swiss stone pine (wingless). The Chilghoza seed is shown with its "articulate wing," which can be removed from the nut (by curious humans) and replaced without injury. The bifurcate base of the wing blade grasps the nut. Most species of hard pine have the articulate wing.

cases of longevity are possible only because the cones of the closed-cone pines remain airtight, and antioxidants contained in the cone scales and seed coats keep unsaturated seed oils from becoming rancid.

Pine cones vary greatly in size and weight. The minute cone of Mugo pine (*Pinus montana, var. mughus*) may be less than one inch in length and one inch in diameter, whereas the sugar pine cone may be one and a half or two feet long and four inches in diameter. In weight, pine cones vary from less than a quarter of an ounce (again in Mugo pine) to more than two and a half pounds, as in the Coulter pine of California.

Pine seeds also vary greatly in weight. Jack pine and lodge-pole pine seeds number about 131,000 and 135,000 per pound, respectively; Coulter pine seeds number 1300 to 1400 per pound, and Torrey pine only 500.

Old Age

Old age comes to pines as to all living organisms. Their life-span is generally long, but some species live much longer than others. Relatively short-lived Monterey pine is already old at sixty or eighty, although it might struggle to reach over one hundred years. The longevity of sugar pine may extend to five

This bristlecone pine (*Pinus longaeva*), known to be more than 3000 years old, grows near the top of Mt. Washington, Humboldt National Forest, Nevada. Bristlecones once formed vigorous forests but now exist in only a few remote areas in the western and southwestern United States. The world's oldest known living thing is a bristlecone pine. (*Dana K. Bailey*)

hundred years or even more, and bristlecone pine has an estimated longevity up to five thousand years.

Much more important than age is the vitality of the species. Some pine species are senescent; they have lost their capacity to expand, to evolve. They are on their way out, still lingering in isolated spots of their once extensive range. Foxtail pine and bristlecone pine are apparently senescent.

But some pine species are vigorous, expanding and evolving. Ponderosa pine is one of them; Scots pine is another. There are many other young and aggressive pine species. Some pines of a restricted distribution might possess the capacity of a vigorous species but have no opportunity to use it. Monterey pine, when helped by man, reveals its wonderful vigor.

Old trees are like old people—the infirmities of aging are upon them. They have difficulties with respiration; its rate in old pines is much lower than in young ones. The annual shoots are not so vigorous as they once were. Although the tip shoot of a very old pine is chronologically as old as the tip shoot of a young tree, the protoplasm of the old tree is not young any more. It is easy to root tip shoots taken from a young pine tree, but it is extremely difficult to do so with shoots taken from a tree that is several hundred years old.

The weakening cambium activity is reflected in the formation of fewer and fewer cells, and the annual rings become narrower. As the old pine grows even older, dead branches appear on it in ever-increasing numbers. The recuperative capacity of the old tree is impaired, and its wounds do not heal so well as before. Its resistance to insects and to fungal, bacterial, and virus attacks is lowered.

The needles become smaller and no longer look healthy, now lacking the luster of youth. Their moisture content decreases. The old pine finds it more and more difficult to provide water for its vital functions. The inflow of food to the growing points drops, and various growth hormones cannot be transported in sufficient concentration to the places where they are needed.

Death

Pines may die at any age, and causes of death are numerous. Pine seedlings may succumb to the attack of a nasty fungus, young trees may die as a result of blister rust, and mature trees may be killed by hoards of needle-hungry caterpillars or by bark beetles.

Sometimes pines are infested by mistletoe, a flowering plant whose place in botany manuals is between the two respectable families of the elms and the sandalwood. Mistletoe is a parasite.[12] Although it possesses green leaves and presumably could photosynthesize and live independently, mistletoe prefers to extract food from the host tree. One or two mistletoe clumps do not harm a pine, but many take too much food from the host and smother its foliage, eventually weakening the defenseless tree. Insects do the rest.

Fire may kill the pine. A direct effect of fire on pines is obvious, but there are also indirect effects. Heat may injure the succulent inner bark. Fermentation of sugary sap may start by wild yeasts, and its alcoholic fragrance may attract insects. Smoke of a forest fire may contain physiologically active gases—acetylene, for example; it may force premature opening of dormant buds in spring and cause their death by a subsequent frost. (See chapter 4 for the ecological role of fire in the life of pine forests.)

Often pines die of old age as old people die. When a senescent, infirm tree is broken by snow or shattered by lightning, the cause is evident. But often the cause of death is obscure, or at least complicated. A drought may weaken the tree, and then it may be fatally attacked by insects or fungi. Whatever the calamity, its roots lose their grip of the soil, the tree cannot resist for long the force of wind, and it falls, returning to the earth from which it came.

The pine is dead. But even the ancients knew that where there is death for a tree there is also resurrection. Look at an uprooted old pine, dead and prone on the forest floor. Its bark, undermined by beetles, is falling off in pieces. Lichens and moss cover its upper side. Its needles are shed, its branches broken. But now observe the dead trunk more closely. Snow packs against it in winter, providing more water for a longer time next summer. Squirrels and chipmunks make their burrows under the log and bring fresh mineral soil to the surface. In the

12. "Parasite" is a Greek word, originally meaning dinner guest!

fall they bring pine seeds to their nests and spill some around. Summer comes, and all along the decaying tree grow pine seedlings, young and vigorous. They have everything there by the log—moist mineral soil, shade, and humus. They are protected from trampling by wild animals, cattle, and people. The old tree is replaced by the young generation.

2

The First

2oo Million Years

*

THE FORESTS AND GLADES of ancient Greece were the home
of nymphs and dryads and of many minor male gods, including Pan himself. Among the nymphs was Pitys, whose duty
was to tend pine trees. She had a lover, Boreas, god of the north
wind, a big burly fellow. He was all right, but oh, how different
he was from gay, flute-playing Pan! Pitys flirted with both.

One day, Boreas asked Pitys what was going on between
her and Pan; her answer was evasive. In their quarrel, Boreas
seized Pitys and tossed her against a rocky ledge. Instantly she
was turned into a pine tree. The resin droplets often seen on the
wounded limbs of a pine tree broken by the north wind are
tear drops shed by Pitys when she thinks of her youth, of her
lover Boreas, and, most likely, of Pan. There grows now on the
Black Sea coast of Caucasus a pine named *Pinus pityusa* to com-
memorate poor Pitys.

In reality pines are much older than the time of classical
Greece. They appeared on the earth late in the Triassic period
of the Mesozoic era, some 170 million years ago (see table 1),
when there were neither flowers growing in the valleys nor
broadleaf trees in the hills—just giant horsetails, tree ferns, and

primitive conifers—the progenitors of pines. It was the age of water and land reptiles, including all kinds of dinosaurs. Some primitive mammal-like creatures had begun to creep around, but their future was as yet uncertain.

TABLE 1

DEVELOPMENT OF PINES THROUGH GEOLOGICAL AGES
(To Be Read from the Bottom)

CENOZOIC ERA. Duration 60 to 75 Million Years.
  Quaternary Period.
    Recent epoch estimated at 25,000 years. Pines expanded and formed large forests in the northern hemisphere.
    Pleistocene epoch, lasting one million years. Four major glaciations. Many pine species perished in the North. Advance in Southeast Asia. Man appeared (?).
  Tertiary Period. Development and further expansion of pines in the northern hemisphere. Toward the end, climate worsened; cold killed many species.

MESOZOIC ERA. Duration 167 Million Years.
  Cretaceous Period. Pines already separated into hard pines and soft (white) pines.
  Jurassic Period. Age of gymnospermous palm-like cycads. Pine fossils are found in several places.
  Triassic Period. Horsetails, tree ferns, conifers. Possibly pines evolved at the end, about 180 million years ago.

PALEOZOIC ERA. Duration 370 Million Years.
  Permian Period. From 280 to 230 million years ago. Aridity in northern hemisphere. Conifers prominent. Araucarias and pre-pines.
Conifers originated 100 million years earlier. Life appeared in seas about two billion years ago. No living organisms have been found in the first three billion years of earth history.

The appearance of pines was not so sudden and romantic as the Greek poets imagined. It has taken nature millions of years of hard and persistent work to create the pine tree as we know it. Physiological and ecological evidence indicates that pines developed on high plateaus and mountain slopes in a temperate climate characterized by alternating seasons of growth (summer) and rest (winter). Geographic and paleobotanic data suggest that pines originated in the North, most likely in the broad landmass known as Beringia, which, prior to the middle of the Tertiary period, connected Alaska intermittently with northeastern Siberia but now is submerged under the waters of the Bering Sea.

We learn the history of pines by studying their fossils. There are uncertain reports that fossil pine pollen occurred in the Triassic deposits but no other fossil pine material of that time has been found. As it takes time for a newly developed tree to reach places where plants may become fossilized—usually at the bottom of lakes—several million years passed before pine foliage, cones, branches, and occasional chunks of wood were deposited in the sediments of the Jurassic period.

Jurassic pine fossils, however, are rare. Pines occurred singly or in small groups here and there, intermingled with other trees. Pines were growing in the mountains, and their remains had to be carried to the deposit sites of the lowlands by cascading streams; thus, pine material was battered and damaged, often beyond recognition. Sometimes their appearance was so uncertain that scientists, studying the fossils in sedimentary rocks, called them not pines but pre-pines.

Only during the Cretaceous period of the Mesozoic era did fossil pines become more common in the deposits of the northern hemisphere, from the islands of the Arctic to the middle latitudes. No fossil pines have been reported south of the thirty-second parallel, and none are found in the southern hemisphere. During the Cretaceous period, about 100 million years ago, pines already had separated into two large groups—hard pines and soft, or white, pines. Even that early in their history many pines were surprisingly similar to the present-day species.

During the Jurassic and, chiefly, the Cretaceous periods, pines spread from Beringia to Siberia, eastward across America, and then, via Greenland and Iceland, to northern Europe, including the adjacent Arctic archipelagoes. But the main trek of pines was southward, along both sides of the Pacific. The migration was slow and tortuous. It has taken pines millions of years to reach the present limits of their distribution. Sinking earth crust and encroaching seas divided continents, and then those continents were united again; climate changed repeatedly; deserts were formed and, later, again became lush; mountain ranges appeared only to be eroded later to a peneplain. Even the north and south poles shifted from one place to another.

Pines had to adjust themselves genetically to the changing environment, and to wait until the way would open again for their migration. During the Cretaceous period, a sea divided eastern and western North America, all the way from the Arctic to the Gulf of Mexico. From that time on, pines moved southward by two routes, eastern and western, and eventually reached Mexico and Central America. A Tertiary sea that separated Europe from Siberia also affected pine migration and their present distribution.

Many more geological changes have taken place during the life history of pines. The Tertiary period was the time of further southern expansion and the rapid evolution of pines, but, during the second half of the Tertiary, the climate of the world became colder. In what is now the Arctic region, pines suffered from cold and gradually disappeared. Even farther south, in western Europe and in Asia, many pine species succumbed to cold. Mediterranean pines, protected by the Alps and by other Tertiary ranges farther east, were not affected.

The Tertiary period ended with chills, and then arrived the great Quaternary glaciation. A mantle of ice, reaching several thousand feet in thickness, covered much of North America and Europe. To the lowlands of northern Europe the ice moved both from Scandinavia and from the Alps, killing everything, including pines. Only in a few sheltered places, or "refugia," did two or three species of pine survive. In the dry Siberian climate, glaciation was not extensive because there was not much moisture in the air for the formation of ice. Pines were destroyed in that part of Asia not by advancing ice, but by the cold, which during glacial times was even more severe than now. In America ice covered Canada and descended in the west to about twenty miles south of Puget Sound, in the east to Pennsylvania, and almost to the confluence of the Mississippi and Ohio rivers.

But even in Alaska and the Yukon Valley there were places free of ice that served as refugia for lodgepole (*Pinus contorta*) and jack pine (*Pinus banksiana*), which survived the glaciation. Generally, however, pines retreated south along the Appalachians before the advancing ice. After the glaciation, lodgepole pine in the west and jack pine in the east returned north and rapidly reoccupied the areas laid bare by the retreated ice. Red pine and white pine followed.

In the southern part of the United States, the Tertiary pines continued to grow, little disturbed while glaciation ravaged the North. The Tertiary relics are especially conspicuous in California; among them are Torrey pine, sugar pine, bristlecone pine, and others.

Pines penetrated Mexico early in the Tertiary along the coastal ranges, but the central Mexican plateau, notoriously volcanic, became available for pines only after the middle of the period when the volcanoes somewhat quieted down. Apparently it was only during the Quaternary period that pines formed forests there and expanded to Central America.

In eastern Asia the story of pine migration and evolution (for the two are inseparable) was different from that in other parts of the northern hemisphere. In the northern parts of East Asia there was no glaciation such as that which occurred in comparable latitudes of Europe and North America. Still lingering in Asia are rare conifers, survivors of the Tertiary period, and among them are some pines (see chapter 4).

At the time of the Great Glaciation so much water had been frozen to form the ice mantle in the north that sea level was lowered all over the world. Shallow straits dried out; islands became peninsulas or formed larger islands. Along the mountain ranges some pines moved down the Malay peninsula and crossed the equator in Sumatra. It is impossible to tell if pines penetrated the other islands of Indonesia because no native pines are found there, and, in the humid and hot climate of the equatorial lands, no pine fossils have been preserved.

Two pine species now growing in the Philippines provide evidence that pines came there via the Malay-Sumatra route and then reversed their southerly advance, turning north and reaching the Philippines. They are Benguet pine (which ap-

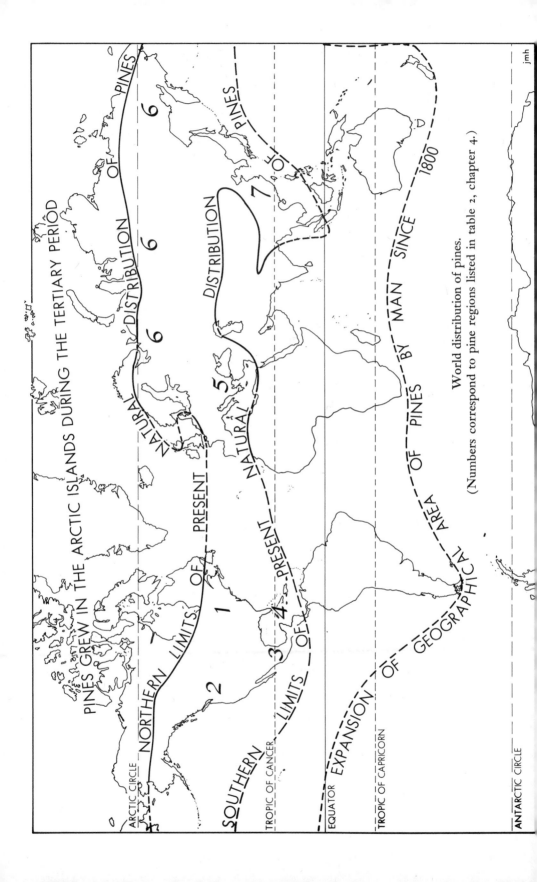

World distribution of pines.
(Numbers correspond to pine regions listed in table 2, chapter 4.)

parently is the same as Khasi pine of the mainland) and Merkus pine. They could not have arrived directly from the mainland across the deep and wide South China Sea. Among other instances of reversed migration of pines is the Tertiary movement of pines north in the eastern United States, or of pinyon pines in the American Southwest.

Shortly after the glaciation pines spread over the remainder of the northern hemisphere, except in deserts and tundra, but they never regained their former habitat in the Far North. Now only three pine species are found above the Arctic Circle.

3

Recent Times

∗

W HILE PINES were advancing slowly southward, man appeared on the earth. Like the pines, he also had taken
millions of years to develop and to spread his kind.

Man encountered pines in many places of the northern
hemisphere. In contrast to the deciduous trees that shed their
leaves—apparently dying—every fall and developed new foliage
every spring, the evergreen pines appeared eternal. Their green
needles in winter were reassuring. Only evergreen oaks rated as
high as pines with primitive man, who worshipped pines as he
worshipped other wonders of nature that he could not under-
stand. For him pines were mysterious and fearfully divine; they
had to be propitiated.

In the beginning pines were worshipped for themselves;
later they became the abode of gods and spirits. When man became civilized, formed nations, built temples, and appointed
priests, he continued to worship pines as the most sacred of trees.
George James Frazer tells us: "The Delphic Oracle (in Greece)
commanded the Corinthians to worship a particular pine tree
'equally with the god (Dionysius),' so they made two images
of Dionysius out of it, with red faces and gilt bodies. . . . In the
art a wand tipped with a pine cone is commonly carried by the

god or his worshippers because the pine tree was particularly sacred to him."[1]

The pine cone appeared on many ancient amulets and had a phallic meaning. It is said that the pine cone was used most in the cult of Venus. Pine cones were regarded as symbols of fertility, and even now the tops of wooden bedposts are often embellished with carved pine cones.

Frazer tells us further that at the festival of Demeter, the Greek goddess of the fruitful earth and happy marriage, pine cones were offered "for the purpose of quickening the ground and the wombs of women." Assyrian priests on ancient bas-reliefs are shown offering pine cones to the altars of gods. Pine cones on these carvings and on the tips of priests' staffs appear to be those of Italian stone pine (*Pinus pinea*), the best the Mediterranean could offer.

Not only cones but the branches and pines themselves were held as objects of veneration. We learn from Frederick T. Elworthy that "The pine tree was sacred to Zeus and an attribute to Serapis. It was beloved of virgins. . . . The *Pinea corona* was the emblem of virginity, which Daphne took from Chloe and placed upon her own head. Among the Romans the chaste Diana was crowned with a chaplet of pine."[2] Because pine was so important and sacred, the Roman poet Ovid referred to pine branches as cut from *arbore pura*, a pristine tree.[3] The pole of Bacchus is described by Roman writers as an inflammable and fragrant pine pole.

Frazer relates that in an ancient Phrygian legend Attis, lover of Cybele (mother of gods), was changed into a pine tree after his death. The cult of Cybele was adopted by the Romans about two centuries B.C., and the sacred pine tree became an object of worship during an orgiastic spring festival in Rome each year on the twenty-second day of March. A pine tree was cut in the woods (most likely *Pinus pinea* or *Pinus nigra*) and

1. George James Frazer, *The Golden Bough,* Vol. 1, 3d ed. (New York: Macmillan, 1935), p. 278.

2. Frederick T. Elworthy, *The Evil Eye* (New York: Macmillan, 1958), pp. 97, 235.

3. Ovid, *Fasti* II, 24.

carried into the sanctuary of Cybele, where it was worshipped. The trunk was then buried. Three days later "the divine resurrection was celebrated with a wild outburst of glee."

In Scandinavia and in northern Russia, the spring festival is held at the end of June. All these festivals celebrate the resurrection of life after its long suspension in winter.

Pines have been, and perhaps still are, believed to possess supernatural powers. The anonymous author of *Cultus Arborum* wrote the following:

> The pine was supposed by some to be inhabited by wind spirits, like Ariel, owing to the whispering noises proceeding from it in the breeze. The legend was that it was the mistress of Boreas and Pan, an idea acceptable to the German mind in consequence of its holes and knots, which were believed to be the means of ingress and egress for the spirits. It is told that a beautiful woman of Småland, who was really an elf, left her family through a knot-hole in the wooden house-wall. "Frau Fichte," the pine of Silesia, is believed to possess great healing powers, and its boughs are carried about by the children on Mid-Lent Sunday, adorned with coloured papers and spangles; it is also carried with songs and rejoicing to the doors of stables where it is suspended in the belief that it will preserve the animals from harm.[4]

Frazer, paraphrasing a German author, tells us: "In some parts of Silesia the people burn pine rosin all night between Christmas and the New Year in order that the pungent smoke may drive witches and evil spirits far away from house and household . . . while young fellows are rendering this service to the community, the housewives go about their houses . . . chalking tree crosses on every door, no doubt to accelerate the departure of witches."[5] Not long ago in Siberia a similar ritual was performed at the Epiphany when crosses were made over every door with smoke of pine torchwood to protect the houses and stables from evil spirits. Later, votive tapers became a more

4. Anonymous. *Cultus Arborum* (privately published 1890), pp. 75–76. *Fichte* in German means "spruce," but Anonymous and Elworthy insist it is meant to be "pine."
5. Frazer, *The Golden Bough*, Vol. 9, 3d ed., pp. 164–65.

convenient instrument for this ritual, which still is practiced by some Russian Orthodox priests and housewives.

In Mexico and Central America, pines were worshipped by the Indians a long time before the Spanish conquest. The Aztecs considered *Pinus teocote* the pine of the gods, and burning its incense-fragrant rosin as an offering in the temples was the privilege of priests and kings. ("Teo" in the name *Pinus teocote* resembles the Greek word *Theos* ("god"), but it is a coincidence.)

In the highlands of Guatemala, Mayan Indians avoid, even now, the killing or harming of pines because they are considered not only living but also animated beings. For household use and for their pagan-Christian ceremonies, the Mayans lop the side branches of pines, leaving a sizable tuft of foliage on the top of the tree so that it will continue to live. An example of present-day reverence for pines occurred in the experience of two foresters known to the authors. While they were driving in the mountains of Guatemala they saw a felled tree trunk lying in the ditch. When they asked their Mayan driver what kind of tree it was, he answered: "When she was alive, she was a pine tree."

The Buriats, a Mongolian people living around the southern end of Lake Baikal in East Siberia, often viewed Scots pine groves as sacred. These "shaman forests" were scattered over dry grassland. Before the Soviet revolution of 1917, one approached and rode through the groves in silence lest the gods and spirits of the woods be offended. Solitary trees near the Buriat villages were always sacred and adorned with talismans, ribbons, or sacrificial sheep skins. These trees were always called pines, although some were actually larches. Beliefs and customs of the Buriats may have changed during the last fifty years. Or have they?

Early American colonists expressed their affection for the pine tree by making it the emblem on historic flags. In 1775 both the Continental and the Pine Tree flags were decorated with the green, conical shape of—no doubt—the eastern white pine. Today the Vermont state seal bears the likeness of a pine tree with fourteen branches representing the thirteen original states and Vermont. And, at present, Maine is called "the pine tree state," where white pine is the official tree and appears on both the state seal and the state flag.

Machado described well the effect of a pine forest on men: During the day the forest appears majestic, the old pines with their crowns way up in the sky, their naked roots clinging to the rocks. At night the forest is filled with mysterious noises, and tree trunks take the shapes of grotesque monsters.[6] One is inclined to keep silent while in a pine forest and prefers to cross it before darkness converts it to the abode of evil spirits.

While worshipping pines, man also learned of their practical uses. The edible, nut-like seeds of the pine cone probably were used for food even by primitive people; they still are eaten in many parts of the northern hemisphere. To quote Frazer again, "wine was brewed by the Romans from *Pinus pinea* seeds and this may partly account for the orgiastic nature of the rites of Cybele, which the ancients compared to those of Dionysius."[7] Mukaddasi, an Arabian historian, wrote that, in the tenth century, pine nuts were a notable product of Syria.[8] No doubt those were Italian stone pine nuts. The tribes of Siberia gather nuts of Siberian white pine, Siberian dwarf pine, and—in the southeastern part of the country—Korean white pine. Russian settlers in Siberia also gather nuts from Siberian white pine and from them press oil, which they call "nut oil." Before the introduction of sunflower, cottonseed, and corn oil (all three from America), the pine nut oil was important in Siberia, where it was considered a delicacy. Before the revolution of 1917 it was used for cooking during Lent when animal fats were taboo.

Indians of the southwestern United States, California, and Mexico also use pine nuts for food. In that part of the continent grow several species of pines: Digger, Coulter, sugar pines, and seven or eight pinyon pines, all having large, edible seeds. Pinyons, which have the largest seeds of all the pine genus, thus provide a good supply of protein-rich food. Even in other parts

6. Antonio Machado, *La Tierra de Alvargonzalez*. The "pines of old Castile" described in the ballad are Scots pines.
7. Frazer, *The Golden Bough*, Vol. 1, 3d ed., p. 278.
8. See Marvin W. Mikesell, "The Deforestation of Mt. Lebanon," *The Geographical Review* 59 (January 1969): 1–28.

of the continent, where pines bear smaller seeds, they are used by the Indians. According to G. M. Dawson, Shuswap Indians of British Columbia collect cones of various sorts of pines and eat the seeds which they extract from them.[9] Pines with fairly large seeds growing in the southern part of the province are ponderosa pine, western white pine, and, rarely, whitebark pine and limber pine. Lodgepole pine grows all over the province, but its seeds are too small for human consumption.

At present several pine species provide nuts for the American food industry: domestic pinyon and Italian stone pine (both have oval seeds), and, to a certain extent, east Himalayan chilghosa pine, which has long, boat-like seeds with one sharp end.

When man settled and learned how to make fire and pottery, he noticed that pines could be useful to him in many other ways. Their pitchy wood made good kindling.[10] Later the wood was used for torches in religious and civil processions, for heating and illuminating homes, firing clay pots, and cooking food. Pine pitch also was—and still is—used for healing wounds. Early in the last century pine kindling (loo-cheé-na) was a common source of light in Russian villages during the long wintry evenings.

When man learned to build boats, pine pitch became an important commodity. At the time of the Flood, God ordered Noah to build the ark and said unto him, "Make thee an ark of gopher wood; rooms shalt thou make in the ark, and shalt pitch it within and without with pitch" [Gen. 6:14]. The likely source of pitch available for this job was Aleppo pine. And it was good.

The Roman statesman and poet Ausonius mentioned tapping pine for resin in Aquitania, in southeastern France. We now call that pine French maritime pine. Possibly it was Austrian pine

---

9. G. M. Dawson, "Notes on the Shuswap Indians of British Columbia," in *Proceedings and Transactions of the Royal Society of Canada, Transactions,* section ii (Montreal, 1892), p. 22.

10. Ovid mentioned pine kindling in his *Metamorphoses* (I: 658): "Et tíbi ego ignárus thalámos taedásque parábam" ("[although] unknown to thee, I have prepared [for thee] a couch and kindlings"). Here *taeda* meant pine torchwood; it was used later by Linnaeus for the name of American southeastern loblolly pine, *Pinus taeda*, not particularly a pitchy species.

(*Pinus nigra*), which occurs now in the Cévennes regions. Columella, a native of Cadiz, Spain, who lived in the first century A.D., noted that pine pitch was used for purifying wine and for treating wine casks. In Greece, pine resin is added to some kinds of wine, called *retsina*.

Apparently pine resin, or pitch, was used in California long before that territory became a part of the United States. Padre Arroyo, an inventor and grammarian who wrote a vocabulary of the Indian languages, even linked pine trees with the naming of California. He told Mr. Evans, an officer of Captain Beechey's expedition in 1826, that the name "California" was a corruption of the Spanish word *colofon*, meaning resin, and that it was suggested by the numerous pine trees that produced it around Monterey, the old Spanish capital.

So much pine pitch (resin) was used in shipbuilding by the British Royal Navy that pitch products—tar, rosin, and turpentine—became known as "naval stores," the name still used to designate the pine rosin and turpentine produced in the southeastern United States. The other important center of pine resin products is in southwestern France. Many other countries are engaged in the naval stores industry, notably Spain, Russia, and Greece. Man extracts resin from pines wherever they grow. Today naval stores are used for making many commodities such as printer's ink, varnishes, food-flavoring extracts, floor wax, camphor, menthol for cigarettes, and lilac-scented perfumes.

Telling about all of man's uses of pine wood would be a big project. The most important products are lumber, plywood, and pulp from which paper and cardboard are made. It suffices to say here that in the United States pine wood, especially soft (white) pine, is used only for fancy interior work and cabinet-making. The job of building houses is relegated to other conifers, chiefly Douglas fir of the Pacific Northwest.

Pine forests, especially the white pines of New England and the Lake States, were vitally important in speeding the early development of the United States. It was loggers who built most of the railroads into the wild forests, thus opening the country to settlers and expanding industry at the same time.

Probably the Chinese were the first to paint pines on panels and silk scrolls to decorate their homes. Later, pine forests or individual trees became a favorite subject of many artists in many countries. The Renaissance painters used pines as the background for their lovely madonnas or as illustrations for stories, as Botticelli did with the Ravenna pines. European art galleries are abundant with Victorian paintings of Scots pines. In every Canadian art museum can be found recently painted pictures of pine forests. In the Ottawa Art Gallery there is a landscape depicting a clear-cut hillside; all virgin white pines are gone and the vigorous young ones are filling the canvas. A cut-over mountainside is a difficult subject to paint, but it has been done well. It is a picture of a regenerated forest.

Poets also shared in describing the beauty of pines, sometimes confusing them with firs or spruces. All of us get elated and emotional as we stroll through a pine grove on a hot summer day when the old trees fill the air with their pungent fragrance. Big bonfires made of pitchy pinewood have a peculiar mystic fascination. As we sit watching the sparks going up, and as we inhale the fragrant smoke, we are inclined to become philosophi-

This wedding-chest panel painted by Botticelli illustrates a Decameron tale and also reveals the fifteenth-century use of a forest of Italian stone pine in Ravenna, Italy. Some trees have been cut for lumber, the branches of others have been trimmed for fuel, and, *left*, tents have been set up by campers. Rabbits and deer represent wild life. (*El Prado Museum*)

cal or to sing nostalgic songs. In "Kavanagh," Longfellow wrote beautifully of "Piny odors in the night air." We are all poets when we are in the pine woods.

It was inevitable that when man, the tiller, moved to live near pine forests, he should begin destroying them to clear land for cultivation and to procure wood for his needs. Sometimes he removed forests because they harbored wild animals and hostile natives. In some parts of the world, pines were destroyed early in the history of mankind. Gone are the original forests of western Europe. Pines once grew in Holland and Denmark, and in Ireland pine stumps are excavated in peat bogs, but no natural pine forests exist today in these countries. None are in England, but the native *Pinus sylvestris* survived in a few places in Scotland and thus it is known as Scots pine even though it grows all over Eurasia, from Spain and Norway across the continent to Siberia and Mongolia.

In America the destruction of pine forests began as soon as the country was colonized. The Crown, striving to preserve the white pine forests of the Northeast for the needs of the Royal Navy, blazed the best mast trees with the "broad arrow," and imposed heavy penalties for cutting the marked trees. Nevertheless, destruction of the forests continued. The colonials preferred to cut the mast trees and to sell them to riverside mills, or even to ship them to countries unfriendly to England. Thus a struggle ensued in a remote part of the realm between law and trespass, between the interests of the British Empire and the activities of a colony.[11]

After the revolution, the forest destruction went on uncontrolled and gradually spread over the country. Toward the end of the nineteenth century the northeastern part of the United States was so intensively logged that the virgin stands of valuable white pine had already disappeared. Still, cutting was continued on the lands which fell out of cultivation after the Civil War, and fine natural stands were produced on rich soil. Their exploitation was extensive and highly profitable.

11. See Joseph J. Malone, *Pine Trees and Politics: The Naval Stores and Forest Policy in Colonial New England, 1699–1775* (Seattle: University of Washington Press, 1964).

In colonial days, America's tallest and straightest eastern white pines (*Pinus strobus*) were marked with the "broad arrow," which indicated that they were reserved for masts in the British Royal Navy. Extending from the Atlantic coast as far west as the Lake States, eastern white pine played an important role in opening wild forested regions for settlement. (*U.S. Forest Service Photo*)

Gradually, lumbering operations spread to the Lake States, to the South, and to the West. In the South, where the climate is warmer than in New England and the pine forests regenerate faster, the damage was not so disastrous as in the North. The Southeast gradually became a center of the naval stores, and later of a thriving pulp and paper industry.

Today, virgin pine forests are rare in America, except in the West. One may find uncut stands of lodgepole pine and western white pine in the Northwest and adjacent parts of Canada, and, occasionally, original forests of ponderosa and Jeffrey pines in the mountains of California. Apparently no more virgin stands of white pine (*Pinus strobus*) remain in the United States. In the Southeast, where not so long ago the folks talked about "old growth" and "second growth" pines, most of the virgin stands also are gone.

In reconstructing the occurrence of original pine forests in an area where they no longer exist, it is common to consider the names of settlements or landmarks indicating that pines once existed there. If in Mexico you repeatedly encounter places called "ocotal" (*ocote* is the Indian name for pine), but you see no pines around, you may assume that pines once grew there but have been destroyed by men. Often this method works well, but sometimes it can be misleading. For example, "The Pines" is the name of the poet Swinburne's residence in Putney, a suburb of London. This does not indicate that pines grew there in the not-too-distant past; Swinburne's place received its name from its gate posts topped with ornamental pine cones.[12] Numerous "Pine Crests" may never have had pines, and heaven knows how many summer homes surrounded with hemlocks and spruces have been named "Whispering Pines"!

So it has been like this, from the days of Rome to our time, that man has destroyed pine forests where, in his opinion, they were abundant. So ruthlessly did he do the job that he has acquired the reputation of a destroyer of natural resources. But now, when virgin commercial stands are nearly gone, man has at last ceased to be a destroyer and has become a planter.

12. *The New Yorker* (January 23, 1971).

4

The World of Pines

*

O NLY RECENTLY has man begun to study the relationship of wild trees to their environment. In 1873 the term "ecology" appeared in botanical books. Originally spelled "oecology" (and still so by the Oxford Dictionary), it is a Greek word meaning the biological economy of plants, or animals, or, simply, the relation of organisms to their environment. Foresters were the first to investigate the ecology of wild trees, and thus was born the science of forest ecology.

We must say a few words about the capacities of pines in responding to environment. The paleozoic ancestors of pines grew during the extremely dry Permian period. They responded to the aridity by developing xeromorphic structures designed for drought resistance: narrow, rigid leaves with a small surface-volume ratio, sunken stomata, leathery cuticle, and waxy bloom. Thus pines started their Mesozoic career well prepared to cope with drought, although, because the Triassic period in the northern hemisphere was milder than the Permian period, there was no immediate need for that. They also inherited physiological drought resistance and could withstand water shortage when need arose.

When, with the advent of the Tertiary period, the skies cleared of misty clouds, the sun became bright, and the Mesozoic air dampness decreased, the inherited drought-resistant characteristics of pines and their endurance to the relentless sunlight served them well. The grotesque, Mesozoic, tree-like sigillarias and cordaites disappeared, and giant horsetails degenerated into mere little plants of swamps, but pines survived and continued slowly but surely their evolution. They developed new and useful traits to meet the ever-present challenge of Mother Nature, whose ways are not always motherly and often are outright cruel. Ecologically, pines became good xerophytes, sunworshippers, drought-enduring and remarkably flexible. Their drought resistance also proved to be lifesaving when some of them were forced to high mountains, because drought resistance also enhanced their resistance to cold.

Throughout the Tertiary period, pines continued their evolution and spread widely over the face of the earth. But pines still were not numerous; they merely intermingled with other Tertiary species, conifer and broadleaf, only occasionally forming small groves alone. The time had not yet come for pines to reach their prominent place in the landscape of the northern hemisphere.

Pines suffered much in the North during the Quaternary glaciation, but in the South they continued their march towards the equator, taking advantage of land bridges formed between islands of southeastern Asia in the Old World. In the western hemisphere, pines reached Central America. (It is well to remember that the Quaternary glaciation, which lasted from one to two million years, was really a series of glaciations, with warm interglacial periods between. It is entirely probable that we are living now in one of the interglacial periods. Some parts of the world—Greenland, for example—are still covered with a thousand-foot sheet of Tertiary ice.)

With the melting of ice after the last glaciation, pines revealed another important trait; they became pioneers, the first to invade and to colonize the unoccupied land left behind by retreating ice. In Eurasia the invaders were Scots pine and occasionally Siberian white pine. In America the pioneer invader in the West almost always was lodgepole pine; in the East, jack pine, and, to a certain extent, red pine (*Pinus resinosa*) or eastern white pine (*Pinus strobus*). Even now pines always are ready to invade available areas denuded by sea, burned by fire, or abandoned by impoverished farmers; loblolly pine of the American

Southeast is still called "old field pine." Other pines also have the same tendency to move into vacant land.

Habitats

In their Quaternary expansion, pines have shown well their ability to adapt to infinitely variable habitats. Because they originated in mountains, even now they prefer mountain slopes of moderate elevation, but some pines have climbed into high mountains. Foxtail pine of California grows at 12,000 feet above sea level; bristlecone pines (*Pinus aristata* and *Pinus longaeva*) form prehistoric-looking groves on arid mountains in the western and southwestern United States at 10,000 to 11,000 feet. Four-thousand-year-old veterans, half-alive, are found on even higher slopes.

One Mexican pine (*Pinus hartwegii*) forms fair forests on the slopes of volcanoes Popocatepetl and Iztaccihuatl at 8000 to 11,500 feet, and approaches the line of permanent snow at about 12,500 feet. On the Sierra Negra, near the volcano of Orizaba, another Mexican pine (*Pinus rudis*) tops them all, climbing to 13,000 feet of altitude. On the other hand, some pine species descend to the sea. In the eastern United States all pine species have their lower limits at sea level. On the West Coast only four or five grow near the ocean.

In Mexico and Central America all pines grow in the mountains with the exception of the Caribbean pine of British Honduras and Nicaragua, which is growing both in the mountains and along the Caribbean coast. It is still questionable whether the Caribbean pine of the coast and that of the interior mountains of British Honduras are of the same species. They look alike, but are they ecologically and genetically the same? Sometimes the external appearance of pines is deceiving and fools many a good botanist.

At the beginning of the Tertiary period, there were no mountains between the present state of Nevada and the Pacific. The climate of the Great Basin at that time was mild, and several California pines grew there. Then the Sierra Nevada began to rise, slowly but steadily, still rising and occasionally shaky in its growth pangs. The rising Sierra intercepted rain-bearing clouds, and the climate in the Great Basin grew drier and drier. Pines either had to adapt to the arid climate, move away, or die. Pinyon pines proved to be the toughest; they remained in the semideserts of the Great Basin. Gradually they spread and adjusted themselves to the arid environment. Those of Nevada became singleleaf pinyons; others developed into the two-needle pinyons of Navajo country in Colorado, New Mexico, and Arizona. Still others became the three-, four-, or five-needle pinyons of northern Mexico, adjacent parts of California, and Utah. Whitebark, bristlecone, foxtail, and limber pines escaped to the high mountains. But sugar pine, western white, and some other, extinct pines perished and are found in the Great Basin only as fossils.

The altitudinal range of some pine species increases from north to south. For instance, Scots pine in northern Europe grows at sea level, whereas in the Mediterranean area it is a mountain tree. Limber pine grows in North Dakota at 3300 feet of altitude, whereas in Colorado it goes up to 12,000 feet. There are many similar examples but also many exceptions, and thus generalization is difficult. Besides the latitudinal influence (it is warmer in the south than in the north), genetics is also involved. Lodgepole pine growing on the California coast is genetically different from the lodgepole pine of Alaska or of the high Sierra.

THE TALLEST PINES

ONE MIGHT ASSUME that the farther south the better pines grow. It is not so. The optimum of pine development is located not in Central America or in Indochina; pines there are not exceptionally big and often are inferior to the more northern pines. It is in California, somewhat expanding beyond the state boundaries, where the tallest pines grow.

There, on the west slopes of the Sierra Nevada, are found the three giants of the pine family: Jeffrey pine, ponderosa pine, and sugar pine. Of the three, sugar pine is the tallest and the biggest, reaching 230 feet in height and almost 10 feet in diam-

Giant of the pine family is the sugar pine, which grows on the western slopes of the Sierra Nevada mountains. It may reach more than 200 feet in height and measure 9 feet in diameter. (*U.S. Forest Service Photo*)

eter. Ponderosa and Jeffrey pines are not far behind. The tallest ponderosas are probably those of the Siskiyous of northern California and southern Oregon.

A long time ago, Dr. Frits Went, discoverer of the growth hormones (auxins), said that pines of the Sierra Nevada of California are tall and big because the growing period there is long, the days are warm and inducive to photosynthesis, the nights are cool, and respiration is not excessive so that calories are conserved and used for building the bodies of the pines. Nobody yet has proposed a more plausible explanation.

THE OLDEST TREES

THE TALLEST PINES are not the oldest. That distinction goes to the bristlecones, and among them are individuals older than any other known living things on earth. Bristlecones are scattered in the most desolate, bare, high mountains of the Rocky Mountains of Colorado, in the Great Basin (eastern California, Nevada, and Utah), and in small areas of Arizona and New Mexico.

Until recently all bristlecones were believed to belong to one species, *Pinus aristata*. Then in 1970, after a thorough investigation, Dr. Dana K. Bailey showed that the Colorado bristlecone and the Great Basin bristlecone are decidedly different, albeit closely related.[1] He renamed the Great Basin species *Pinus longeava*.

The estimated maximum attainable age of *Pinus longeava* in Nevada and California is five thousand years. In southern Utah, where the bristlecone grows occasionally as a forest tree in company with other conifers and where there is slightly more rain, the estimated age is three thousand years. Dr. Edmund Schulman, who studied the resistance to adversity exhibited by these trees at their highest elevation, wondered whether they might "serve as a guidepost . . . to understanding longevity in general."[2]

1. D. K. Bailey, "Phytogeography and Taxonomy of Pinus Subsection Balfouriana," *Annals of the Missouri Botannical Garden* 57 (1970): 210–49.
2. See David Muench and Darwin Lambert, *Timberline Ancients* (Portland, Ore.: Belding, 1972), p. 63.

In 1964 one of these incredible bristlecones was cut down. Studies of its annual rings convinced scientists that it was at least 4844 years old and could have been older than 5000 years. The death of the gnarled, misshapen ancient was so widely noted and mourned that bristlecones are now guarded jealously by the U. S. Forest Service. At present the oldest known living individual on earth is a 4600-year-old bristlecone pine, appropriately named Methuselah, growing at an elevation of 9500 feet in Schulman Grove in the White Mountains of California.

The nearest relative of the distinguished bristlecone is the foxtail pine (*Pinus balfouriana*), which grows sparsely in northern California at about 7000 to 8000 feet, and more densely in the southern Sierra Nevada at about 8800 to 12,000 feet. It has an estimated longevity of only about 1000 years.

PINES IN THE NORTH AND IN THE TROPICS

NORTHERN PINES have one thing in common with all far northern wild life: as with fish in the arctic seas and water fowl of the arctic coast, there are not many species among them, but the number of individuals in each species is enormous. This holds true for geese, ducks, and other arctic sea birds; for fish such as salmon, cod, or herring; and for northern pines—Scots pine, jack pine, or lodgepole pine.

On the other hand, in tropical latitudes there are many species of fish, birds, and pines but few individuals in each species. In the tropical highlands of Mexico and Central America there are more pine species than in any other regions of the northern hemisphere, but the number of trees in each species is small in comparison with the northern forests.

The abundance of arctic fish and water birds has been attributed to the presence of more oxygen in cold water, hence more plankton—a staple food for fish—hence more birds. But we are not yet able to explain the multitude of trees and scarcity of species in the northern pine forests. As there has so far been no urgency for forestry to inquire into this fascinating problem, it remains one of those interesting puzzles for young forest researchers to tackle.

REGIONAL DISTRIBUTION OF PINES

PINES GROW all over the northern hemisphere; one species even spills over the equator. They can be grouped into seven regions, each having its distinctive features, as shown in table 2.

It is certain that new pines will be discovered in the future, most likely in Mexico, Central America, and in eastern Asia, and some known pines will be renamed and reclassified. For example, there is a pine species in southern Vietnam (*Pinus krempfii*) which does not look like a pine; it is so new to science that it has no common English name. Krempf pine may give us a clue to the predecessors of true pines.

Whereas world distribution of pines is generally well known, only those species which have economic value have been studied ecologically and physiologically.

ECOLOGICAL GEOGRAPHY OF PINES

WIDE DISTRIBUTION of a pine species does not mean that the species is the same throughout its extensive area. Often a species has to be subdivided into subspecies, varieties, ecotypes, and "physiological races."[3]

Scots pine grows in the plains and lowlands of northern Europe, where it rains in summer and snows in winter, and on the slopes of the Alps; it covers the tops of the Spanish Sierras and the mountains of the Caucasus, where climate is relatively mild; and it occurs in the arid steppes of northern Mongolia, where summers are dry and winters desperately cold but almost snowless. A pine cannot remain biologically and ecologically the same under all these diverse conditions. In the forest zone Scots pine prefers dry sandy soil and acts as a drought-resistant xerophyte, but in the southern grasslands it clings closer to the rivers, where there is more moisture, and behaves as a mesophyte, that is, a species growing in places of balanced moisture.

---

3. This term originated in Australia, where it was found that some eucalypts look alike but differ in the chemical composition of their essential oils and thus in their physiology.

TABLE 2

Regional Distribution of Pines

	Pine Region	Number of Species	Regional Characteristics
1.	Eastern North America	13	Large forests in the north and south. Scattered in between. Little variability. Mostly at low elevations. Some in moderate mountains.
2.	Western North America	20	Large forests in mountains. Scattered in arid places. Some up to 12,000 feet elevation; few at sea level. Not much variability. Tallest pines and oldest pines.
3.	Mexico, including Central America	31 plus	Medium-size forests on the continent. None at sea level. Upper limit 13,000 feet. Great variability among hard pines. Taxonomy not always well known. More will be described in future.
4.	Caribbean Area	4	Scattered at sea level of various islands. One species grows up to 9000 feet elevation.
5.	Mediterranean Area	12	Some in mountains; others at sea level. Often difficult to say whether native or planted. Canary Island pine, Mugo pine, and Swiss stone pine are included in this region.*
6.	Northern Eurasia	3	Large forests. One species merely a shrub. From low elevations up to 5000 or 6000 feet.
7.	Eastern Asia	24 plus	Large forests in north; otherwise scattered. Some at low elevations. Four species go above 10,000 feet. The rest are of moderate mountains or at sea level. Variability in white pines. Some pines not yet well identified.
	Total	107 plus	Exact number of species cannot be given because most likely more pines will be described in the future

* Swiss stone pine is included in the Mediterranean area arbitrarily. On climatic grounds it should be placed in the region of northern Eurasia.

The ubiquitous Scots pine as it appears in the Caucasus mountains of the U.S.S.R. Scots pine is the most widely distributed pine in the world. (*A. G. Dolukhanov*)

Ponderosa pine grows not only on the coastal ranges of the Pacific, where it crosses several ecological zones of the Sierra Nevada, but it is found also on the plateaus of Arizona, in the Rocky Mountains, and even in the Black Hills of South Dakota, thus growing in the regions of different soils, different temperature ranges, and different rainfall patterns.[4] Generally, ponderosa pine is subdivided into the Pacific coast variety and a Rocky Mountains variety, but the subdivision should perhaps go deeper. The Black Hills ponderosa and the Arizona ponderosa, although both belonging to the Rocky Mountains variety, are biologically different pines.

It happens occasionally that a pine species changes gradually and imperceptibly into another pine species, and in the area of their contact it is difficult to say which is which. Such is the case of northern Chinese pine (*Pinus tabulaeformis*), which in its southwestern limits gradually changes into Yunnan pine (*Pinus yunnanensis*) and forms a confusing overlap zone where pines go by the name of *Pinus densata*.[5]

Even in the same locality, ecological conditions might vary enough to cause the existence of physiological races. For example, the whole west slope of the Sierra Nevada of California, from foothills to high mountains, is clad in ponderosa pine forests. It is the same species all over; yet, when its low-elevation strain is planted in high elevations, the trees suffer from cold and don't grow as well as they do at lower altitudes. At the same time, the transplanted trees of high altitudes do not take the whole advantage of the warmer climate at low elevation, and do not grow as well as the native trees do. Growth of pine trees at a given location is influenced by both heredity and environment.

Sometimes a pine species occupies a large area and still looks uniform. Such is Chinese *Pinus massoniana*. No varieties of this pine have been described by botanists. Neither are there named varieties of red pine and jack pine of North America. Possibly closer examination would reveal variability in jack pine.

Some pines are restricted to a particular environment. White-

4. The Sierra Nevada range has been divided by the California botanist Jepson after Merriam into several "Life Zones": Lower Sonoran, Upper Sonoran, Transition, Canadian, Hudsonian, and Boreal.

5. Wu Chung-Lwen, *Acta Phytotaxonomica Sinica* 5 (1956): 131.

Blending well with a small shrine perched on a rocky cliff in northern China is this stand of Chinese pine (*Pinus tabulaeformis*) at an elevation of 3500 feet. Widely distributed and extremely variable, this species is found most abundantly in northern and north central China. (*Arnold Arboretum*)

Top:
Lodgepole pine at an elevation of 8600 feet, straight and timberlike.
Bottom:
Lodgepole pine at timberline at 10,000 feet, scrubby and trailing.
Both photographs were taken in the San Jacinto mountains of
California. Lodgepole is sometimes called tamarack pine. (*U.S.
Forest Service Photo*)

bark pine is a multistemmed, small tree, usually of the alpine habitats of the West. It is a better-looking tree in the North. The singleleaf pinyon is a species of the arid Nevada slopes. Mexican Nelson pinyon (*Pinus nelsonii*) and Pince's pinyon (*Pinus pinceana*), both yielding large, edible nuts, are found only in a few spots of the Mexican northeastern desert ranges. Digger pine is an untidy, strange-looking but lovely tree of the scrubby, chaparral-clad foothills of California mountains.

Also restricted to California are several other pines of limited distribution. Coulter pines grow exclusively in the dry coastal ranges of the southern part of the state. Torrey pine occurs only in two small groves on the coast near San Diego and on the nearby island of Santa Rosa. Monterey pine is found on the mainland in three patches, one near Monterey and the other two north and south of it, all three localities facing the Pacific. Unexpectedly, it also grows on Guadalupe Island off the coast of Mexican Lower California.

Along the California coast, almost from Oregon to the border of Mexico, grows Bishop pine, not continuously but in several small, much-culled groves. Pines of all these groves, except the bluish-needle strain of the extreme north, look alike, but they don't intercross. Each grove behaves as a different species.

On the dry coastal ranges of California grows the small knobcone pine, which extends to the more favorable environments of Oregon and up to the Sierra Nevada. In both places it reaches a fair size and ranks as a forest tree, but essentially it is a species of dry chaparral hills.

In the eastern United States, the most prominent pines are, in the North, jack, red, and white; in the South, slash, longleaf, loblolly, and shortleaf pines. There also are scattered secondary species: sand pine, spruce pine, Table-mountain pine, pond pine, pitch pine, and Virginia pine. The Virginia pine recently has achieved important commercial status.

In their ecological behavior, eastern pines differ much from western pines. There are no giants in the East comparable to those of the Sierra Nevada, and no alpine species. Often when eastern pines are transplanted to the West they don't grow as well as they do at home, where they enjoy summer rains. On the other hand, California coastal pines die of the sudden cold waves so common in the southeastern United States.

In Mexico and Central America, pine forests occupy a prominent place on the central plateau. They are not so extensive as in the north, but they contain many strikingly beautiful pines such as *Pinus montesumae*, *Pinus pseudostrobus*, and *Pinus lumholtzii*.

The benign climate of tropical Mexico and its diversified topography have been exceptionally favorable for developing new species of pines. Their continuous intercrossing has produced varieties, and the varieties have intercrossed among themselves to create more varieties, some of which would in time become new species. It is often difficult to tell in Mexico where one pine species ends and the other begins.

In scientific parlance, a secondary center of evolution and speciation of pines has been formed in the Mexican highlands. It is a real headache for a conservative botanist to identify pine species in Mexico, because the pines there do not behave as good Linnaean species should; they interbreed too freely.[6] A European plant collector, Roezl, who visited Mexico in 1815, listed in his catalogue about one hundred species of Mexican pines; most of his "species" are not valid.

In the Caribbean area, *Pinus cubensis*, *Pinus caribaea*, *Pinus tropicalis*, and *Pinus occidentalis* are scattered on the islands of the Bahamas, Cuba, Hispaniola (Haiti and the Dominican Republic), various cays, and along the Atlantic coast of Central America. The first three are lowland pines, and the fourth is a mountain species that grows in the sizable forests of Hispaniola Island.

In the Old World, pines are distributed as unevenly as in America. In the Mediterranean area, Aleppo pine and Pityusa pine cling to the coasts. Others climb to the mountains, where they form fine forests of Austrian pine (*Pinus nigra*) with its wide ecotypic variations or Macedonian white pine (*Pinus*

6. Carl Von Linné (Linnaeus), who in 1753 proposed a classification of plants and gave to every plant its specific name, believed that all species have been created as such and that they do not cross with other species. His was a time when the laws of genetics and the intricacies of inheritance were not known. As the first step in studying plants, the Linnaean species is still very useful.

Austrian black pine (*Pinus nigra*) growing not far from Vienna in the low Alps, at an elevation of about 1000 feet. Intense care by Austrian foresters keeps the forest in model condition, free of underbrush and dead wood. (*Austrian Forest Research Institute*)

The picture-postcard tree of the Mediterranean is the Italian stone pine, whose unusual shape is an accident of environment—its human neighbors lop the lower branches and use them for fuel. Untrimmed, it looks like other pines. Italian stone pine is a popular planted tree all over the warmer parts of the world. (*Forest Research Institute of Spain*)

peuce). And one pine, *Pinus cembra*, is found in the alpine zone. Only French maritime pine extends to the lowlands of southern France and to the coast of Portugal. *Pinus montana* reaches farther north than any other Mediterranean pine.

The Italian stone pine (*Pinus pinea*) of the low altitudes is the picture-postcard pine of Italy. It was planted for its beauty and for its large, blunt seeds—*pinoli*—even before Roman times. Pinoli are a commercial product, used locally and even exported to America. It is impossible to tell now where *Pinus pinea* is native and where it has been planted. Since Roman times it has been called domestic pine in contrast to the wild pine, *Pinus sylvestris*.

No doubt there were more pine forests in the Mediterranean region in the old days. The Balearic Islands were known by their Greek name, "Pityusae," or Pine Islands, and the Caucasian coast of the Black Sea was called "Great Pithyum."

In northern Europe original Scots pine forests are rare; most of them are replaced with planted, well-managed stands. Farther east, in northeast European Russia, are still many good, if spotted, Scots pine forests, which extend to Siberia and to the lower slopes of its southern mountains, the Altai and the Sayans. The western Siberian alluvial lowlands still have extensive stands of Siberian white pine, which also occurs in the southern mountains. *Pinus pumila* is a trailing shrub which occupies large areas in northeastern Siberia (in Kamchatka bears make long tunnels in the thickets of this pine) and extends to the mountains of Korea and northern Japan.

In Korea, Manchuria, and adjacent parts of Russia grows the stately Korean white pine, usually as an admixture to the Tertiary broadleaf forests. Because of its excellent wood, it has been badly culled and in places almost completely destroyed.

Pinus bungeana, known to the Chinese as "bark-shedding pine," is lacebark pine, which is scattered all over the mountains of central China. There are several other pines on the mainland of eastern Asia and on nearby islands, but their ecology still awaits thorough study.

Because the tropical part of eastern Asia does not possess the climatic and topographical advantages of the Mexican highlands,

Shrubby *Pinus pumila* in central Japan, growing at an elevation of 8860 feet. Dense fields of this pine occupy millions of square miles in northeastern Asia and adjacent islands. It forms important ground cover for the retention of snow and water, and its seeds are edible. Probably an introduced variety, the grouse (*Tetreo parvirostris*) is a common bird in the pine forests of northeastern Asia. (*Yasaka Hayashi*)

no major secondary center of evolution and speciation has developed in eastern Asia. Many white pines grow in eastern Asia, but they are generally restricted to different islands or regions, one vicarious species in each, and there is at present no contact among them.

More Tertiary conifer genera grow in eastern Asia than grow anywhere else: *Metasequoia, Pseudolarix, Keteleeria,* and *Cathaya.* Among them grows the above-mentioned *Pinus krempfii,* whose botanical position is so uncertain that some botanists think it is a different genus, *Ducampopinus.* It is rare; until recently its specimens could be found in only two European herbaria, one in Paris and the other in London. In 1961 complete specimens of Krempf pine were brought from Saigon and distributed among several herbaria in the United States (Gray Herbarium of Harvard; the National Herbarium in

Because of its venerable age, this *Pinus bungeana* in Seoul, Korea, is protected by a fence and respectfully labeled. It is a planted pine more than 400 years old. Picturesque with chalky white scaling bark, wild *Pinus bungeana* is a rare pine of China, and was often planted near temples and in cemeteries. (*U.S. Forest Service Photo*)

Washington, D. C.; University of California, Berkeley; and the U.S. Forest Service).[7]

7. There had been two fragmentary specimens of a few needles (obtained from the Paris Herbarium) on display at the Gray Herbarium and at the Arnold Arboretum, both at Harvard University. By 1961 apparently the specimens had been lost. The Saigon specimens were collected by Vietnamese foresters and brought from Saigon by N. T. Mirov.

If Krempf pine is a pine, it is a strange one indeed. Some of its features are those of white pines; others resemble characteristics of hard pines; and still others such as broad, sharp-ended leaves borne in two's and the presence of wood parenchyma are her own. Krempf pine occurs singly in the mountains of southern Vietnam, near Da Lat, north of Saigon, and by now it may have been blasted out, burned, or defoliated. It must be studied diligently before a proper place is found for it in the botany manuals.

In Indochina, pines are dispersed in small groves throughout the general landscape of tropical evergreen trees, or intermingled with them. Pines growing there are Da Lat pine, related to the Himalayan white pine; an uncertain white pine called tentatively by French botanists "Pin du moyen Annam"; and two hard pines, Khasi pine (*Pinus khasya*) and Merkus pine (*Pinus merkusii*).

During the Quaternary glaciation both Khasi and Merkus pines penetrated via the Malay peninsula to Sumatra and then to the Philippines, where Khasi pine is known as *Pinus insularis*. It is sparingly distributed in the mountains of southeastern Asia from the Khasi Hills of India to southern Vietnam but has disappeared gradually from most of the Philippine Islands. However, in the mountain provinces of northern Luzon it not only survived but formed extensive forests, a strange oasis of northern flora surrounded by tropical lowlands where bananas and Nipa palms grow.

Merkus pine occurs in the Philippines in two places: in Luzon, where it comprises three badly burned and mistreated groves; and in the more southerly island of Mindoro, where it fares better. Merkus pine also survived in the Barisan mountains of Sumatra, where it is found in twelve places still in the northern hemisphere, and, in one spot, at 2° 6′ south of the equator. Little is known about the ecology of Indochinese pines. Thus Merkus is the only pine species now growing naturally in the southern hemisphere. With this exception, all pines are trees of the northern hemisphere; Norfolk Island pine and Hoop pine of Australia are not pines but araucarias.

During the Tertiary period, pines also migrated westward to the pre-Himalayan ranges that extended along the northern

The strange Krempf pine (*Pinus krempfii*) occurs singly in the mountains of southern Vietnam, the only place where it grows. Some of its features are those of white pine, others resemble characteristics of hard pine, and still others such as broad, sharp-ended leaves borne in two's and the presence of wood parenchyma in its wood are her own. The Krempf pine's botanical position is so uncertain that some botanists think it is a different genus, *Ducampopinus*. (*Dana K. Bailey*)

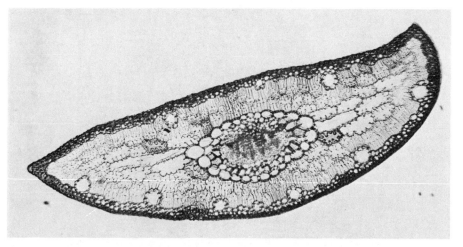

Cross section of a Krempf pine needle from Da Lat, Vietnam. As its central vascular bundle is single, Krempf is more closely related to white pines than to hard varieties. The needle shape is unusual, resembling that of fir. No flat needles are found in any other pine species. The nine holes close to the periphery are resin canals. (*A. G. Johnson*)

coast of the ancient sea to the Mediterranean region. Later these ranges were replaced with deserts, and the Mediterranean pines became separated from the pines of the Himalaya and of the whole of eastern Asia.

The Himalayas' lower southern slopes are today covered with handsome tall forests of chir pine (*Pinus roxburghii*), also known as *Pinus longifolia*. Above these are forests of Himalayan white pine, whose name has been changed several times. For many years it was called *Pinus excelsa;* later it became *Pinus griffithii;* and recently it was renamed *Pinus wallichiana*. Generally it is still known as *Pinus excelsa*. It has close relatives in America, in eastern Asia, and in the Balkans. The third Himalayan species is chilghoza pine of northwestern India, Pakistan, and adjacent parts of eastern Afghanistan, where it sometimes grows together with chir pine, sometimes with the multinamed white pine. Chilghoza pine is a messy, branchy species, notorious for its capacity to invade the abandoned, exhausted fields of impoverished farmers. But it is useful because its boat-shaped seeds, locally called *chil-ghus*, are large and

Khasi pine (*Pinus khasya*) in Thailand grows tall and stately on shallow rocky soil at an elevation of about 4500 feet. No young pines are evident because of repeated fires. (*Thailand Forest Service*)

sweet. The seeds are exported to the United States, where they are preferred by confectionery makers because they are easier to stick into cakes and sweets than are the blunt, native pinyon pine nuts or the Italian *pinoli*.

THE NORTHERN AND SOUTHERN BOUNDARIES

To SAY THAT the northern limits of pine forests are dictated by extreme cold in the arctic region is only partly correct. It is

These handsome chir pines of the Himalayas in Nepal present a dense, softened outline because of their long needles, sometimes measuring 12 inches. The species, *Pinus roxburghii* (*Pinus longifolia*), grows in the foothills and mountains up to an elevation of 6500 feet. (*U.S. Aid Mission to Nepal*)

not the low winter temperatures that prevent pines from growing in the northern tundra along the Arctic Ocean; winters are
colder farther inland, in the forest zone, yet pines survive there.
It is the coolness of the short, arctic summer, the closeness of
permafrost (frozen ground) to the soil surface, and strong, dry-
ing winds that prevent the expansion of pines northward.

After glaciation, pines never regained their former habitat in
the Far North. Now only three pine species are found beyond
the Arctic Circle: *Pinus sylvestris* and shrubby *Pinus pumila*
grow as far north as 70½° latitude; the third, *Pinus sibirica*,
barely crosses the Arctic Circle in western Siberia. No pines are
found north of the Arctic Circle in America.

In the Old World, the southern limits of the present distribution of pines on the mainland are in southern Vietnam, Cambo-
dia, Thailand, and Malaya. Merkus pine is an exception.

Causes determining southern limits of pines in the Old World
are many. In the Mediterranean area, in the Levant and in northern Africa, the southward extension of pines was checked by
low rainfall, low air humidity, high air temperature, and excessive soil salinity.

The advance of pines in southeastern Asia was stopped by
the hot and humid climate of the lowlands of India, monsoon
rains, and perhaps by human activities. Farther south, toward the
Indian Ocean, are the mountains of the Malabar coast of India, of
Orizza, and of Ceylon, where pines could grow well, as shown
by recent pine planting. But pines simply had no chance to mi-
grate naturally to those places. Westward lie the deserts of
Afghanistan, Central Asia, Iran, and Arabia. Pines had no chance
there, either. East of India, conditions for the southward expansion have been more favorable. The mountain ranges of Indochina permitted pines to expand farther south, where the
vanguard hard pines were Khasi and Merkus pines. The afore-
mentioned occurrence of Merkus pine in Sumatra is the only
reminder of a more southern distribution of pines in southeastern
Asia during the Quaternary glaciation.

In the New World, the southern limit of pines is in Nicaragua. The pioneer species there are two hard pines: *Pinus oocarpa*
of the highlands; and *Pinus caribaea* of the Caribbean coasts and
islands. Of the two, the Caribbean pine has been more successful

in advancing toward the equatorial lowlands. *Pinus oocarpa* still lingers on the slopes descending toward the Lake Nicaragua lowlands, hot and powder-dry in one part of the year, hot and humid in the other. Pines arrived in Nicaragua so recently, possibly in historic time, that they have had no time to cross the lowland and establish themselves in the mountains of Costa Rica on the other side of Lake Nicaragua. An unusually strong wind or a migratory bird could carry pine seeds over the lowland, but either the seeds just have not yet been transported to Costa Rica, or the seedlings there have not survived.

When man arrived, the southward advance of pines in Central America not only was checked but was pushed back by the burning of mountain slopes for grazing and cultivation. Two white pines have penetrated Central America: Mexican white pine and Chiapas pine, the latter still considered by conservative botanists as a variety of *Pinus strobus*, which grows more than two thousand miles away. In Central America, it reaches Guatemala, whereas Mexican white pine extends to Honduras and to northern El Salvador, latitude about 14° north.

DIVERSITY OF PINE FORESTS

WITHIN THE LIMITS of the area occupied by pines, their distribution is determined by their relation with the environment. Since the environment is different in different parts of the world, many different types of pine forests exist. For example, some forests such as those of ponderosa pine in Arizona, Scots pine of Eurasia, or Benguet pine of the Philippines consist of only one species. Other forests are composed of several pine species such as the magnificent stands of ponderosa, Jeffrey, and sugar pine in the Sierra Nevada of California, where, in so-called mixed conifer forests, one or two pine species grow alongside a true fir, Douglas fir, and incense cedar. In the Black Hills of South Dakota, ponderosa pine shares its environment with birch, and, in East Asia, Khasi pine is admixed to the tropical, broadleaf evergreen (selva) forests. *Pinus oocarpa* occurs in the selva forests of Central America, and Korean white pine is a prominent component of Manchurian hardwood forests.

The low foothills of California mountains are covered with chaparral, a scrubby confraternity of various shrubs, among which are scattered strange Digger pines with their gray-green foliage, and occasionally the humble knobcone pine. In the southern part of California the rare Coulter pine might be found amidst the chaparral. These scattered pines can barely be called forests. As yet they are little known ecologically, and the relation of the pine to the chaparral brush is complex. It is known that when fire destroys the trees they are replaced by chaparral, but it is extremely difficult for the pines to retrieve their former place in the chaparral community. Similar pine associations exist in the Mediterranean area, where chapparal is known as maquis and the pine is Aleppo.

After the Quaternary glaciation, pine forests expanded over large areas in the northern hemisphere and formed many different forest types. The sum of all pine communities—a pine forest—plays a definite and important part in the vegetative mantle of the earth. Among all other geographical landscapes such as forest, woodland, grassland, or desert, be it in mountains or in lowlands, pine forests occupy a conspicuous place. Explorers and geographers never fail to describe them as a component of geographical landscapes. Pine forests are a geographical phenomenon.

5

The Pine Forest

*

A s THERE ARE many species of pines and many different environments, every pine forest has its specific ecological
pattern, or "ecosystem," a term proposed in 1935 by the English
philosopher-ecologist, Sir Arthur Tansley. By this term Tansley
meant "a system (in the sense of physics) including not only
the organism-complex, but also the whole complex of physical
factors forming what we call the environment . . . the habitat
factors, in the widest sense."[1]

Gradually "ecosystem" came to mean a natural community
where inorganic and organic components interact so precisely
that a stable, if delicate, system is created in which matter and
energy circulate as in a single organism. Many other terms such
as "facies," "bioms," or "forest type" have been used to describe
the ecological nature of plant communities, but lately "ecosystem" has become almost universally accepted.

A pine forest is a complex ecological system in which atmospheric, inorganic, and living components work together in
a delicate equilibrium. If a single component is removed or al-
tered, the whole ecosystem is affected. When everything goes
well, the forest behaves as an orderly Tansleyan ecosystem.

We already have seen that the northern and southern limits

1. A. G. Tansley, "Vegetational Concepts and Terms," *Ecology* 16 (1935):
299.

of pine distribution, as a whole, are determined by climate. Obviously, climate also is the most important environmental factor in pine distribution and in pine ecology within the boundaries of different pines. But climate has not been the same all the time. Remember that, when the benign, warm period of the first half of the Tertiary became colder and colder, and culminated in the Quaternary glaciation, many pines disappeared completely and the distribution of the others changed. But even minor fluctuations of climate—droughts, floods, hurricanes, late frosts, and unseasonable snow—may cause many changes in a pine forest.

Northern species migrated south and became genetically changed to frost-tender pines; when transplanted back to northern localities, they often suffer from cold and succumb to subfreezing temperatures. There is no general rule, however. Each pine species behaves differently, and some are more frost-tender than others.

The tolerance of pines to extremes of heat or cold is remarkable. Northern pines (jack pine or red pine) may tolerate temperatures as low as $-60°$ F and lower; the Siberian pines can stand even colder weather. It all depends on whether or not the pine has the inherited capacity to drain the water from its living cells into the intercellular space. If a pine has this capacity, coupled with proper timing, it can withstand cold. If not, it suffers or even dies.

On the other hand, some California pines of low elevations (Digger pine or knobcone pine) and the Aleppo pine of Libya on the African coast of the Mediterranean survive where summer temperatures may rise well above $100°$ F. Fortunately, the transpiration of these pines keeps them somewhat cooler to maintain cell protoplasm below the coagulation point of cell proteins, which is about $133°$ F. When the inside temperature of a pine passes that point, the pine dies. Death can occur if no more water is available for transpiration.

Water is delivered to the forests as the result of solar radiation, which causes water to evaporate from the oceans, form clouds, and return to earth as rain or snow. Solar radiation also provides light necessary for photosynthesis. With radiation come cosmic rays—some from the sun, others from far beyond. Neutrons, protons, and electrons clash, disintegrate, and bombard our pines to cause changes or mutations in their chromosomes. Some of these changes are harmless or unimportant; others contribute to the evolution of pines and their never-ending adjustment to the changing environment. Still other mutations are outright harmful; they may interfere with the orderly process of inheritance, contribute to pine abnormalities, or cause defects in their progeny.

When pine species grow in areas of deep snow, like the Sierra Nevada of California, where snow measures to a depth of thirty-five feet, young or stunted pines may be buried under it for six months or more. More snow is retained in a forest than in the open because wind velocity is slower within a forest than without. In the spring, the accumulated snow melts slowly and penetrates gradually into the soil, keeping the soil damp for a long time.

In northwestern Siberia and in adjacent parts of the Japanese archipelago, the trailing *Pinus pumila* is covered with deep snow for a long winter. Its pliant branches bend close to the ground at the advent of winter and straighten up again when the snow is gone in summer, in some places as late as August.

Very little study has been done of the winter life of pine ecosystems where trees are covered with snow. Pines are dormant in winter. Soil does not freeze under deep snow, and possibly roots do not cease their growth during the winter. But in the darkness, buried pines cannot photosynthesize. Experiments that were made with the dwarf form of *Pinus cembra* in the Austrian Alps, where snow is deep in winter showed that respiration of buried pines still goes on but at a much slower rate. Nonetheless, the effect of snow on pines is a fascinating problem still awaiting a thorough investigation in a pleasant alpine environment.

Pines vary in their tolerance of sea salts in the air. Some species such as Torrey, Monterey, or Bishop pines of the Pacific coast of California, and Aleppo pine of the Mediterranean, grow too close to the open ocean. Wisely, they stop some distance from the water lest they be subjected to the salt spray. Eastern white pine on the coast of New England is extremely susceptible to salt spray; during severe hurricanes salt spray might be carried for many miles inland and damage pine foliage. Planted Austrian pine in the same area is more resistant to the effect of the spray. Possibly other pine species such as those of the cays of the Caribbean Sea or pines of the small islands off Japan also are more resistant to salt spray than are the inland pines.

Soil is an extremely important ecological factor for plants, but it is not absolutely necessary for them. Plant life originated in water, and there still are many plants—small and large seaweeds, and even some flowering plants—living in water. Pines can be grown in water if adequate amounts of minerals are added to the water. But, because pines are terrestrial plants, they are geared to grow on solid ground and be satisfied with what is available from the soil.

Soils vary from one place to another, and pines throughout their long evolution adjusted themselves to different soil types and various degrees of soil moisture. Siberian white pines grow well in the broad valleys of western Siberian rivers, thriving on the soil enriched by spring floods. In the mountains of California, lodgepole pine grows in bogs and on dry flats and slopes. Whitebark pine lives on granite; bristlecone pine grows on dolomite (carbonates of calcium and magnesium). Austrian black pine tolerates lime soil, whereas French maritime pine cannot stand it. The ubiquitous Scots pine occurs on chalk deposits in southern Russia, on acid soil in the North, and in poor, sandy areas where other trees cannot survive. California Digger pine is exceptionally tolerant to serpentine soil, supercharged with magnesium and several minor elements.

Either too much or too little moisture in the soil affects the well-being of pines. They are xerophytes; they cope with a shortage of water much better than do the freely transpiring broadleaf trees. Only desert plants, cactus and succulents, can do better. Overabundance of water expels air from the soil pores and suffocates pine roots; trampling soil around pines does the same.

In the extreme north of pine distribution, summer sun can be warm enough to cause needles to absorb carbon dioxide from the air while the ground is frozen solid. The absorption of water by the roots is then impossible, and photosynthesis cannot take

Slash pine (*Pinus elliottii*) in northern Florida. Roots of some trees may be submerged all year, but the abundance of moisture doesn't make the trees grow better than pines grown in drier soil. Humid warm air induces the luxurious development of Spanish moss, which is not a moss but a flowering plant.

175 193

place. Photosynthesis is hindered also when stagnant water in bogs becomes supercharged with humic acids, or is lacking oxygen; there is plenty of water in the soil, but it is not available for pines. Such a condition is called physiological dryness of the soil.

Occasionally noxious gases are present in soil pores. The effect of soil gases on pines is little known, but there is no doubt that some gases such as hydrogen sulphide or marsh gas may have a harmful effect on the growth of pine roots. It is known that when respiration of bacteria causes a concentration of carbon dioxide in soil air to a point of nine or ten percent, the soil becomes toxic to pine roots.

When pines grow near the seashore, there is danger of excessive concentration of various salts in the soil: table salt, Epsom salt, Glauber salt, and others.

And yet pines do grow at the seashore, for instance, Scots pine on the coast of the Gulf of Finland, or slash pine on the coast of the Mississippi Sound. But the Gulf of Finland is about as far from the Atlantic Ocean as is Lake Superior, so water in the gulf is almost as fresh as in a freshwater lake. Salinity in the Mississippi Sound is also much diluted with fresh water brought by the great river.

Soil is more than minerals, air, and water; it is alive with all kinds of organisms—bacteria and fungi. The numerous bacteria perform useful functions such as entrapping atmospheric nitrogen or decomposing various minerals.

We already have mentioned that feeding roots of pines are wrapped in fungal threads, thus forming a strange symbiotic combination called mycorrhiza. The ecology of mycorrhiza has been studied well only in the temperate pine forests, where soil is moist and rich in organic matter. But how does mycorrhiza form and function in summer, for instance, in the semideserts of Nevada or Chihuahua, where pinyon pines grow? Mycorrhizal fungi need moisture in the soil and at least some humus, and there is not much of either in the top soil of the arid countries.

Mycorrhiza also needs air to breathe, but sometimes pines grow in swamps with their roots submerged in water. How does mycorrhiza behave when water is not sufficiently aerated?

Opinions differ, and more studies will have to be made before we know enough about this important factor in various pine ecosystems.

Especially important is the ecological knowledge of mycorrhiza when pines are transplanted into places far from their native habitat. There might be no suitable fungi in the soil of the new home to make pines grow normally.

Not all fungi are good enough to form mycorrhiza. Some are harmful to pines. They may attack roots, spreading infection underground from tree to tree; they may kill seedlings and attack young trees. Fungal rot often has destroyed the entire insides of old trees. Cankers on the trunk of an old pine are the fruiting bodies of fungus working inside the tree, a sure sign that its center is rotten.

Some fungi live in the soil by themselves without entering into mycorrhizal relation with pines. They are useful in decomposing dead wood and needles. Then again, some fungi spend all their life (or cycle) above ground, attacking pine trunks, branches, or needles.

Probably the best known fungus is the infamous blister rust, which attacks only white pines. Blister rust came to America from Europe, where white pines are immune or highly resistant to it. In the northeastern United States it has done much damage to eastern white pines. In the western United States it is likely that blister rust came from British Columbia, where it entered from overseas. Spreading to the western white pine of Idaho and adjacent states, it still kills pines there. Foresters are now breeding rust-resistant white pines. The hard pines have their own species of rust. The most serious disease of loblolly and slash pines is a relative of white pine blister rust.

A dense pine forest is almost devoid of birds. You may see an evasive woodpecker or hear the hammering of his drill as he digs for insects. Occasionally you may notice nuthatches climbing up or down (headfirst) pine trunks. Small flocks of chickadees may be passing through the woods, and at night an owl will hoot in the crown of a pine tree. But when pine cones mature in the fall, the forest may be invaded by jays and nutcrackers (*Nucifraga*), which often are useful because they disperse heavy wingless pine seeds that cannot float in the air. Sometimes, however, they consume the entire seed crop. They are especially fond of the pines that have large, wingless seeds such as whitebark pine, Swiss stone and Siberian white pines, limber pine of the Rocky Mountains, and pinyon pines of the American West. The pinyon groves are the nesting home of a special pinyon jay (*Gymnorhinus cyanocephalus*).

In the northern forests of Scots pine, lodgepole pine, or jack pine (species having small seeds) are found crossbills (*Loxia*), which extract seeds from pine cones with cleverly designed, overlapping beaks.

Most birds of the pine woods prefer open slopes, glades, and forest fringes, where there is more light and more vegetation. Shrubbery provides good nesting and abundant food—tender buds in the spring, and seeds and berries in the summer. The air is full of gnats, mosquitoes, and flies. The forest also attracts predators, for instance, shrikes that catch rodents and small birds. And always, in the skies, are hawks, kites, and falcons.

Game birds include various grouse and quails. The European black grouse (*Lyrurus*), sporting a lyre-shaped tail, is notorious for nipping off tender buds in the spring, sometimes causing considerable damage in northern pine forests.

In a well-balanced pine ecosystem, mammals, large and small, play an important part. Rodents churn up forest soil, and mice are useful in spreading the pine seeds. Gray squirrels are conspicuous in pine forests when seeds are ripening. Often they are too impatient to wait until pine cones are mature; they clip off the green cones, only to throw them away half-chewed when they find the seeds unpalatable.

Red squirrels are the most notorious "cone cachers." In the taiga region of Eurasia the culprits are the gray squirrels (*Sciurus vulgaris*), which also, as the most important commercial fur animal, are removed from the forests in great numbers. The Russian geographer Berg wrote in 1946 that squirrels killed in the taiga region totaled fifteen million annually. Unique among the forest animals of Siberia is the mass migration of squirrels from one locality to another. We know that most of these migrations are caused by lack of food, but some still await explanation.

Chipmunks are everywhere in pine forests, exploring every log, climbing every tree, and running to their burrows at any sign of danger, real or imaginary. Bats, although mammals, have more habits in common with birds than with their closer kin, the mice, rats, or chipmunks. Because they are nocturnal, bats prey on insects at night while insectivorous birds are sleeping.

Many other mammals—fox, wolf, coyote, badger, wolverine, lynx, bear, sable, pine marten, weasel, skunk, and others—are the participants of different pine ecosystems of temperate climates. Of the hoofed animals can be found moose (*Alces*), called elk in England but in eastern Siberia, where it is hunted commercially, it is represented, strangely, by *Alces alces americanus*. It is a dangerous animal in the wilderness, but it is perfectly tame and docile when domesticated. The female bears two calves each year.

The stag, or red deer (*Cervus elaphus*), commonly called elk in America, has been exterminated in continental Europe but is found in a few places in the highlands of Scotland and rarely in the Caucasus mountains. In southern Siberia it is replaced almost completely by a wapiti elk (*Cervus canadensis asiaticus*). Even wild reindeer, traditionally an arctic animal, lives among pines in the Sayan mountains of southern Siberia, most likely the region where it was originally domesticated.[2] Deer, called roebuck in Europe, is common in pine forests; close to human habitations where it is safe from predators, it is even on the increase. Other elk and deer species live in pine forests of southern and eastern Asia. All these hoofed animals prefer, as do birds, the meadows and fringes to the dense pine forests. The moose loves swamps.

In prehistoric times wild cattle played an important part in the open woodland type of pine forests by disturbing grassy sod and exposing mineral soil, making it more suitable for the germination of pine seeds. For example, wild cattle helped jack pine in its westward expansion across Alberta, Canada.[3]

In northern dense pine forests, cattle never have been an important ecological component. In the South, grazing is prac-

2. See N. T. Mirov, "Notes on the Domestication of Reindeer," *American Anthropologist* 47 (1945): 393–407.
3. See N. T. Mirov, "Composition of Turpentine of Lodgepole and Jack Pine Hybrids," *Canadian Journal of Botany* 34 (1956): 443–57.

ticed when no better pastures are available, as in the piney woods of the deep South or in the open pine stands of the American Southwest and adjacent parts of Mexico. Moderate grazing does not harm pine forests; it is even beneficial. Cattle loosen the surface soil and bring precious manure for pines.

Sheep and goats, however, are a real menace to pine forests, particularly those of dry southern regions. Sheep clip off everything green, including pine seedlings. Goats are even more destructive. It is said that, because goats can reach higher branches than can sheep, goats are to be blamed for the denuded, once-pine-clad mountains of Greece; they prevented regeneration of trees. Both sheep and goats are grassland or alpine animals; they don't fit into the pine ecosystems.

Snakes, lizards, and frogs are frequent inhabitants of pine woods, inconspicuously doing their share of controlling rodent and insect populations.

Many kinds of insects live in the pine forests; some of them are outright harmful. Various bark beetles attack and kill trees of all ages. Moths, in caterpillar stage, may be disastrous to pines. Gypsy moth infestations in northeastern America occasionally reach an epidemic proportion. A closely related moth of the Old World is equally harmful. A Russian geographer once described an epidemic caused by this moth in a white pine (*Pinus sibirica*) forest of the Altai Mountains in western Siberia. Hundreds of square miles of pines were defoliated and killed by the caterpillars. One could hear the sound of myriads of caterpillars chewing pine needles. Water in the streams was polluted by dead larvae and the stench was hard to bear. Wildlife—sable and gray squirrel—left the infested forest. Fortunately, such infestations are rare.

Not all insects are that bad and many are useful to pines. Some churn up the soil and make it more palatable for trees; others help in the decomposition of dead trees. Mosquitoes, gnats, or various flies provide food for birds, dragonflies, and bats.

Spiders are not so common in pine forests as are beetles, gnats, or moths. Some can be seen running on the ground; others spin delicate geometric cobwebs suspended between trees and designed to catch insects. Even the spiders have their place in pine ecosystems.

Then there are the worms, existing—as do other small creatures—in such astounding numbers of species that they beggar attempts to list them and to explain their places in the order of things.

Because pine forests are not restricted to any particular region, they may enter into coexistence with almost any other trees, shrubs, and herbaceous plants. Other conifers may intermix with pines: spruce or hemlock in the American Northeast; incense cedar in California; larch in Siberia; and at least eleven sundry ones in Vietnam. Broadleaf trees, both the deciduous of the temperate regions and the evergreen of the selva, that is, broadleaf, forests in the humid tropics, may not only admix to pines but also invade the forests and crowd them out. Under the canopy of domineering pines are often found shrubs of various density, large or small, deciduous or evergreen, even in the pine forests of cold countries.

Ground cover in pine forests may be almost absent in some ecosystems but luxurious in others. There may be berry plants, flowering herbs, and grasses. Generally, however, shrubs and ground cover plants occur in the openings where there is more light.

All higher and lower animals and plants found in the various pine ecosystems participate in running the complicated machinery called the pine forest. If some of these participants do more harm than can be tolerated by the ecosystem, other participants usually will control them. Only when disaster strikes—flood, drought, fire, or pollutants introduced by man—is the balance destroyed, and the potentially harmful components of the ecosystem reveal their nature.

And, finally, the main component of the ecosystem is the pines themselves. Usually, in a wild forest, they are of all ages. There are mature, vigorous trees, good cone bearers, and in the openings of the forest are young pines and seedlings. Perhaps also there are veteran trees more than one hundred years old, some already dead and standing as ghostly snags, others fallen and decaying. Foresters call this an "uneven" age stand.

When a wild forest, as described above, is almost completely destroyed by a major disaster—hurricane, flood, or, more commonly, fire—only a few mature trees remain. If the disaster is followed by a good seed year the whole area receives enough seeds to develop an "even" age stand. Trees in the stand may be the same age, but when they reach maturity they look as though they are of different ages. When their growth rings are measured they show variations not in the number of rings but in their width. In trees of the same age one large tree may have broad rings, whereas the next, suppressed tree has rings so narrow that they are difficult to discern with the naked eye.

Whatever their age, the living individual trees of the pine forest always compete with each other. Those with genes for tallness and for vigor have an advantage from the beginning and become leaders of the ecosystem. They overshadow and suppress the less vigorous pines and rob them of soil water and nutrition. Eventually the weaker trees die of starvation.

Foresters divide pines of a forest into five classes: (1) dominant; (2) co-dominant; (3) intermediate; (4) suppressed; and (5) dead. The forest looks like a human society. Dominant and co-dominant trees run the show. They compete with each other for water and minerals and for their place in the sun. Because their roots often intergraft, the trees have an opportunity to share sugars, minerals, and proteins, but root intergrafting sometimes also allows harmful fungi to spread infection by roots from one tree to another. If this happens, the whole forest suffers.

Sometimes a pine ecosystem contains not one but several different species of pine, in which case several species compete and the ecological correlations are more complicated. Usually one species is dominant; the rest are just associates. Variations, of course, are many.

Little is known about pine ecology in tropical latitudes. It is a thrill to see, for instance, a grove of *Pinus pseudostrobus* in southern Mexico or Guatemala, where epiphytes, orchids, and Spanish moss (Tillandsia) grow in the trunk crotches of trees.

Lightning fires occurred in pine forests, of course, even in prehistoric time. Sometimes they were large and devastating, but mostly they were local, as they are now. Fires played a sanitary role because they prevented the accumulation of debris and kept the forest floor clean. When fire was disastrous, nature

Uncontrolled forest fire in Boise National Forest, Idaho. (*U.S. Forest Service Photo*)

had thousands of years to repair the damage and gradually restore the forest and preserve the pines. Fire never exterminated a pine species; only changing climate can do that.

In America, when man settled near pine forests, he began to burn them to clear land for pastures and cultivation. Often fire escaped, turned into conflagration, and not only cleared the land intended for fields but also destroyed man's habitation. Fear of fire appears to be in man's blood. When he had to manage his forest, he tried to protect it from fire lest it become wild and uncontrolled. In doing so, he allowed debris to accumulate in excess and thus not only increased the danger of fire but also interfered with the orderly life of the ecosystem.

In the pine forests of the temperate regions, fire often kills seedlings and saplings, but the older, thick-barked trees survive and quickly reseed the burned area. However, if reseeding is delayed for some reason, other conifers or broadleaf trees and shrubs may invade the area. Later, pines gradually appear in the canopy openings and eventually overshadow and replace the broadleaf species.

When pines regain their dominance, the pine forest ecosystem is restored and the cycle of "plant succession" is completed, but there are many variations. In the North, the stages of plant succession may be long, appearing to be permanent. Ecologists call these stages "terminal communities," or "climaxes." In southern regions, where trees grow fast and succession also is fast, it becomes evident that a climax cannot be considered final and permanent. It is wise not to refer to those pine forests caused by fire as "climaxes," "sub-climaxes," or "fire climaxes" but instead to call them "pine stages" of the fire-caused ecosystems. Nothing is final or terminal in these stages. They depend on the intensity and the frequency of fires, both being extremely variable phenomena.

The effect of fire on pine forests has been observed in many parts of the world. Apparently, at the end of the eighteenth century, the area of longleaf pine in the American Southeast was expanding because Indians burned the grass annually, killing the broadleaf trees, which are more vulnerable to fire than are pines.[4] The present extensive, pure pine forests of the south-

4. Sir Charles Lyell, *A Second Visit to the United States of America* (New York: Harper and Rowe, 1849).

eastern United States are "pioneer communities" that have replaced the mixed broadleaf forests. Man gradually converted the original forests by clearing land, abandoning fields, and (recently) planting trees. These forests are not climax forests but pine stages, artificially maintained by use of prescribed fire, that is, fires deliberately set and controlled. ("Prescribed fire," a term suggested by Inman F. Eldredge of the U.S. Forest Service, was made a catchword by Harold Biswell, professor of forestry at the University of California, Berkeley.)

In Honduras all pine forests are apparently of a secondary origin as a result of clearing and burning broadleaf forests, a practice that goes back to Mayan times. In Indochina pines probably could perpetuate themselves as components of broadleaf-conifer forests without the necessity of forest fire. But in the event of conflagration, pines are always handy to invade and reforest the burned area.

Fires are responsible, if not for the origin, surely for the perpetuation of an ecosystem known as "pine savanna," which means, usually, an open pine forest of scattered trees in the warmer parts of pine distribution that have a more or less pronounced dry period. Fire is a necessary prerequisite for the existence of pine savannas, but not all scattered groves of pines are savannas. For instance, pinyon pines of the arid slopes and mesas of Nevada or Arizona cannot be classed savannas because fire is not necessary for their existence.

At present, pine savannas are the result of burning the land for grazing, but in prehistoric time most likely they were the result of lightning fires. Pine savannas vary in different parts of the world, depending on local climate, topography, vegetation, and pine species. In Central America the participant is Caribbean pine; in the Philippines, Indochina, and Sumatra, Merkus pine is the savanna tree; in Yunnan, China, one of the components of savanna is Khasi pine.

The ecology of pine savanna on the east coast of Nicaragua has been described as follows: When a broadleaf forest (selva) with solitary pines among dominant trees is burned out, pine seedlings appear and the area soon is covered with rapidly growing pines.[5] Gradually, pines mature, and among them selva trees

5. Jeffrey Radley, "The Physical Geography of the East Coast of Nicaragua" (master's thesis, University of California, Berkeley, 1960).

begin to appear. In the next stage of plant succession, pines find themselves overshadowed by selva. Pines gradually disappear; only a few vigorous ones tower over the lush green canopy of the selva. The selva remains dominant until the next fire, when the thin-barked broadleaf trees succumb to heat. The fire-resistant pines survive and disseminate the area, converting it to a pine savanna again.

If man protects a pine savanna from fire, the pine savanna gradually converts to a permanent selva; if the fires are spaced at intervals of five to twenty years, the pines maintain themselves as dominants, and the pine stage becomes a climax.[6] In plant succession caused by fire, pines have shown well their ancestral tendency to invade any territory denuded by glaciation, flood, or fire.

The precision and orderliness of a forest ecosystem has given foresters the idea of applying to its analysis the laws and methods of cybernetics, a science concerned with communication and control mechanisms in machines, robots, and biological systems. The whole life of a pine forest, including the exchange of energy and matter, would be reduced to a mathematical equation, whereby interrelation between various parts of the ecosystem would be determined. Computers then would see to it that the forest is functioning properly.

6. Leslie R. Holdridge, *Curso de ecologia vegetal* (San Jose, Costa Rica: Instituto Interamericano de Ciencias Agricolas, 1953).

6

Man-Made Pine Forests

✳

ALREADY IN the seventh century such was the shortage of wood in southern Europe that the Visigoths prepared a code concerned with the preservation of oak and pine forests. Much later, in 1310, the king of Portugal, Diniz el Labrador ("the Farmer") issued a law to protect pine forests. Large-scale planting of pines started in Portugal in the eighteenth century, and forests of repeatedly planted maritime pine (*Pinus pinaster*) are growing there today under well-organized management. One of those park-like planted pine forests, the well-maintained roads of which are lined with brick-size marble blocks, grows north of Lisbon between the coastal town of Nazaré (which looks like a Van Gogh seascape) and Leiria. The best strain of maritime pine comes from the Leiria forest.

In Italy, during the fourth and fifth centuries, monks introduced the western Mediterranean nut pine (Italian stone pine) to the Adriatic coast of Romagna, partly as a source of fuel and nuts and partly as an ornamental. It was the origin of several large pine forests—*pinete*. The Ravenna *pineta* became famous after Dante extolled its beauty in the *Commedia Divina*. Boccaccio wrote a story about it, and Botticelli illustrated it on four large panels of a wedding chest. (Three of the panels are in the Prado museum of Madrid, and the fourth one was sold at auction in London in 1967.) Byron and Shelley wrote about the Ravenna forest, and Henry James described it in the bitter-sweet prose of "Italian Hours."

The *pinete* are on the decline now. Some have been cut to give place for cultivation; others have been destroyed by fire. The Ravenna forest itself also is deteriorating, and no longer resembles Dante's *pineta*.[1]

Italian stone pine has been planted also in other parts of the Mediterranean area and far beyond. It thrives in California. *La Pineta Clementina* near Rome, planted mainly for aesthetic reasons in 1666 on the initiative of Pope Clement IX, still is maintained. Even in the Arab world of the Mediterranean, pine planting has been going on for a long time. Fakhr-el-din, ruler of Lebanon, is known to have planted Italian stone pine at least three hundred years ago.

The large pine region of Landes is located in Gascony in France. For centuries the region had been known as an unhealthy malarial area of scattered maritime pines and swamps. Along the coast, sand dunes had been moving inland, encroaching on poor pastures overgrazed by sheep. Then in 1801 a great project of afforestation of the Landes began, and now the region is covered with more than a million acres of productive maritime pine, the second largest naval stores center of the world.

Der Grosse Föhrwald of Austria is another example of early planting of pines. The forest was planted by order of Queen Maria Theresa at the end of the eighteenth century. Located between the towns of Wiener Neustadt and Neunkirchen, not far from Vienna, it is small—only about 10,000 acres—in comparison with the pine forest of Landes, but it is the pride of the country. The species planted there is native Austrian pine (*Pinus nigra*).

A curious dissemination of pines occurred in the Moslem world when pilgrims, returning from Mecca to their native lands via the eastern Mediterranean, would pick up some pine seeds to plant in their native villages. Thus *Pinus brutia* can be found

1. Nicholas T. Mirov, "The Pines of Ravenna," *Natural History* 80 (January 1971): 24–26.

in a remote village of Tadjikstan in the mountains of Central Asia. This slender forest tree is a native of the eastern Mediterranean, but it was first described from Calabria, a region of southern Italy known as Brutium in Roman times. Apparently it was planted there a long time ago, perhaps even before the Romans.

In China grows *Pinus bungeana,* the "bark-shedding pine." The bark of this beautiful if somewhat unusual tree resembles that of the sycamore, as it peels off in multicolored jigsaw pieces. Because of its ornamental appearance, this pine has been so widely planted for such a long time that it is impossible to say now where it is native and where it has been introduced. Even recently, at least until the Chinese revolution, peasants would bring from the woods seedlings of the bark-shedding pine in baskets attached to the ends of a long, limber pole, and sell the little pines in the town markets.

One landmark in Seoul, Korea, is an old bark-shedding pine, whose leaning trunk looks freshly whitewashed. It is a venerable tree. A large plaque on its front says, in plain Korean, that the pine was planted in the fourteenth century (see p. 86).

In northwestern Russia one may see along the coast of the Gulf of Finland "ship forests," established by command of Peter the Great in about the year 1700 (and later often transplanted) to provide masts for his newly founded navy. In northern Germany many pine forests have been continuously cut and replanted for a long time.

From the performance of pines planted in botanical gardens, it has been learned that each pine behaves differently and often unpredictably when transplanted from its native land to a foreign country. Because so many local conditions must be considered, each planting presents a special problem. In the Royal Kew Gardens near London, Macedonian white pine of the Balkans thrives, whereas sugar pine of California is stunted, scabby, and does not bear cones. Mexican pines grow well in the Tjibodas Mountain Botanical Garden in Java (elevation 4800 feet), but the few pines planted at sea level in the Singapore Botanical Garden, not far from Java, are a miserable sight.

The most spectacular event in the history of pine planting was the introduction of pines into the southern hemisphere. You

Commercial Monterey pine forest near Rotorua, North Island, New Zealand, ready to be cut for lumber or for pulping. The by-product is turpentine, from which menthol and other products are made.

will recall that, in their steady prehistoric migration southward, pines reached the outskirts of the equatorial lowlands and even crossed the equator in Sumatra during the glacial time. Most likely they would have continued their migration and possibly have reached Australia and New Zealand, but, unaided, they would have had to wait until the continents unite, the seas disappear, and mountain ranges form, as happened in the Mesozoic era and most likely will happen again millions of years hence.

But, with the help of man, pines became recently and in a short time well established in the southern hemisphere. When Australia and the islands of the southern hemisphere were discovered and colonized, the settlers in many places faced a shortage of wood for building their houses. Local forests could not always provide good construction lumber; the native araucarias, cousins of pines, were soon depleted, and they regenerated slowly. In search of a rapid-growing tree, the settlers found, about a hundred years ago, that California Monterey pine is the best. This pine, *Pinus radiata*, in earlier days was known as *Pinus insignis*. In its homeland, it forms a small seaside forest, the King's Forest at Monterey, the old Spanish capital of California (*monte* is "forest"; *rey* is "king"). There also are two smaller coastal groves of this pine, one north and the other south of Monterey. A little sprinkling of Monterey pine is found also on Guadalupe Island off the Mexican coast of lower California. That's all; a few hundred acres all told.

It is a picturesque pine. The old trees with gnarled branches support a dark green crown through which sunrays cannot penetrate. There are beautiful old Monterey pines in the botanical gardens of New Zealand.

One hundred acres of seedlings growing at the Rangiera Forest Nursery, South Island, New Zealand, are a source of supply for the country's intensive afforestation and reforestation program. In New Zealand, Monterey pine is called radiata pine.

But it is not for the stunning beauty of Monterey pine that New Zealanders and Australians selected it. It was because of the remarkably rapid growth in its youth, both in height and in girth, and also because, when harvested, it yielded more wood per acre than any other lumber tree they had tried. Later it was planted in other countries of the southern hemisphere, mostly in Chile and southern Africa. Europe also followed New Zealand and Australia in planting Monterey pine forests. The most recent and successful efforts are the plantations in northeastern Spain.

Introduction of Monterey pine into the southern hemisphere was not always successful. There were difficulties with the formation of mycorrhiza because proper mushrooms were lacking in many places. In Australia, some eucalypts (there are more than five hundred species there) were generous enough to share their mycorrhizal fungi with pines, but more often mycorrhiza had to be brought from the homeland—just a handful of moist, good soil from the native pine woods. Also, there were nutritional difficulties, especially with minor elements such as zinc or molybdenum in Australia, and cobalt in New Zealand.

Pines are invaders and colonizers, but when they are introduced into a new environment, they are forced to participate in new ecosystems and adjust themselves for living together with the local plants and animals. They can stand much direct sunshine, winter cold, prolonged drought, and they are photoperiodically neutral, that is, their "flowering" (reproductive stage) does not depend on the length of days. But one thing they all dislike is the continuous, excessive air humidity of tropical lowlands. It is not their environment.

Plants, birds, and animals apparently are receptive to entering ecological relationships with pines in their new home. It is a surprise to see kangaroos and wallabies browsing in the Monterey pine forests of Australia as happily as in their native eucalypt "bush." And it is a joy to watch flocks of screeching, red and green parrots cracking hard pine cones and eating the seeds—a diet new to them and more palatable than the eucalypt's pungent fruits. Professor John W. Duffield told us that in western Australia the large black cockatoo underwent a major population explosion with the introduction of French maritime pine. Indeed, foresters consider the "cocky" a major nuisance in their efforts to collect seeds for planting. Only one Australian animal, the koala (a marsupial, as are all other native Australian animals, except the Dingo dog), does not accept pines, preferring to eat nothing but the leaves of only certain eucalypts.

In the lowlands of the Australian tropics, however, Monterey pine fails to perform well. As a species of the temperate, albeit mild, climate, it needs winter rest, however short. Its forced continuous growth in the tropical lowlands is detrimental to its health and appearance. Instead of branching, it shoots up a single, needle-covered stem, called a foxtail or rattail, weak and easily broken by the wind. (Some other pines also develop foxtails in humid tropical countries.) That is why, instead of Monterey pine, Caribbean pine is planted on the tropical coastal plains of Australia. Caribbean pine grows naturally closer to the equator than does Monterey pine, and thus performs better in the lowlands of Australia near the Tropic of Capricorn.

Many other species of pines have been planted in the southern hemisphere. In South Africa *Pinus patula*, a species from the high mountains of tropical Mexico, is preferred. Loblolly and slash pine are extensively planted in river valleys of Argentina and in Brazil. Today, almost all countries of the world plant pines, even arid Saudi Arabia. Millions of acres throughout the world are clad now with the planted pine forests. In 1971 in the United States alone, more than a million and a half acres were planted to forest trees, and a good part of this area was planted to pines.[2]

Various methods are used in reforestation of cut-over pine forests and in afforestation of areas where they never have been grown. In a cut-over pine stand, some vigorous "seed trees" are left to scatter seeds around, or seeds are sown by hand, by helicopter, or by airplane. Pine seeds also may be sown in seedbeds like vegetables, nursed there for one or two years, and pampered for one more year in transplant beds. From the forest nursery, the little pines are transplanted to their permanent location.

When one flies over the reforested area, be it in the Lake States of America, or in Germany or Australia, one sees rows

2. U.S. Forest Service, "Forest and Windbarrier Planting and Seeding in the United States," 1971 Report.

A well-managed forest of Scots pine in Sweden, its neatness further enhanced by snow. In cold Sweden a Scots pine takes one hundred years or more to grow to merchantable size. This photograph was taken at an elevation of about 1640 feet. (*Bo Nilsson, courtesy Swedish Forest Service*)

upon rows of planted pines of different ages, like children of a school, from kindergarten up to the senior class, and finally the strips of mature trees. Here and there, in the clearings of the pine forest, are perhaps bright green seedbeds and transplant beds of forest nurseries, bright green because they are well tended and well fertilized. The transplants have to be strong and healthy; after being moved to their final destination, they will be on their own and should be vigorous so that they may become the dominant members of the ecosystem.

When a planted pine forest is well managed, appropriate

thinnings are made and the monotonous straight lines disappear. Only a forester can tell whether it is a natural or planted forest; a layman will find joy and beauty in both. By regenerating pine forests man amply repays the sins of deforestation. But he has done more. Without realizing his achievement, man within the last two hundred years has expanded the geographical area of the genus *Pinus* to the entire southern hemisphere, a task that would have required unaided nature millions of years.

FORESTERS AS PINE BREEDERS

WHEN FORESTERS began to plant pines, they would go to the woods, gather cones of wild pines, extract seeds, and sow them. To be sure, they attempted to harvest seeds from good-looking trees, trees that were tall, straight, and not too limby. And in scores of years, sometimes centuries, by gradual, painstaking selection or by sheer luck, they occasionally achieved good results. (The Leiria strain of maritime pine, mentioned above, is a good example of the development of superior strain from wild trees.) Generally, however, from the days of King Diniz to about fifty years ago, foresters perpetuated wild plants with all their uncertain genetic traits, good and bad.

In the agriculture of civilized countries, the practice of gathering seeds of wild cereals, vegetables, and fruits was discarded early. All our staple cereals had been domesticated, selected, and much improved at least ten thousand years ago. Today, the gathering of pine nuts, berries, or North American wild rice (which is not a rice species) is no more than a fancy for gourmets who consider them delicacies. Real gatherers inhabit only the remotest nooks of the earth, and even there the gathering of wild plants for food is often a matter of custom rather than of necessity.

On the contrary, the gathering of wild seeds in forestry is still practiced, although collecting seeds from the best-looking pine trees has not always been successful because there is no assurance that the tallest and straightest pine will produce tall and straight offspring. The pollen parents were not known to the forester, and the seed parents often looked elite not because of noble birth but, as with people, because of exceptional opportunity, which, for pines, means sufficient nitrogen for the roots and light for the crown.

During the ages of agricultural domestication, cosmic rays created many useful mutants; the plants intercrossed, and their chromosomes doubled and quadrupled, thus forming tetraploids and polyploids. Nature put rich genetic material at the disposal of man, who used all these gifts of nature without knowing their intricacies. When, at the beginning of this century, the Mendelian laws of inheritance became known, they were a real boon to agriculture but not to forestry. Virgin forests still existed; they appeared inexhaustible and self-sustained. Although the most valuable pine stands of western Europe were already gone and the shortage of good lumber was already felt, there still remained plenty of Scots pine in eastern Europe and even more pines in Siberia and in North America. The abundance of pine forests provided no incentive for the genetic improvement of any forests, pine or others.

It is true that, even in the last century, pine forests of Europe were well managed, but it was a management not of domesticated but of wild trees. Forestry was based not on Mendelian but on Darwinian principles; the forester's job was to help nature in the survival of the fittest trees in their struggle for dominance. By removing undesirable, inferior species and suppressed trees, the forester provided more light and more nutrition for those pines which he designated as dominant. He cared little whether the good qualities of his selected trees had been caused by their noble origin or by favorable environment. Those were the days when lumber was cheap, competition keen, and any expenditure for improving forests, higher than a few cents per acre, was prohibitive. Who would have been so reckless as to invest in the breeding of forest trees?

Foresters also were aware of the difficulties. They knew only too well that, in theory, Mendelian principles could be applied to forestry. But there was a great difference between, say, cereals that complete their life cycles from seed to (improved) seed in one summer, and a forest tree that takes years and years to mature. The difficulties appeared to be insurmountable. In the North, in Germany or in Scandinavia, where forests are well managed, it takes one hundred years or more to grow a merchantable Scots pine.

And yet the impact of genetic laws on forestry had been growing. Early in this century in Europe and in the United States modest experiments were made in the breeding of cotton-

The late James G. Eddy, founder of the tree-breeding station now known as the Institute of Forest Genetics, Placerville, California, stands between a hybrid and a nonhybrid tree. *Left:* The hybrid, a lodgepole (*Pinus contorta*) crossed with a jack pine (*Pinus banksiana*). *Right:* A lodgepole pine. Both trees are from the same seed-tree and both are 14 years old. (*U.S. Forest Service Photo*)

Administration building and laboratory of the Institute of Forest Genetics at Placerville, California. The Institute is a field station of the Pacific Southwest Forest and Range Experiment Station, U.S. Forest Service, Berkeley, California. (*U.S. Forest Service Photo*)

woods. The breeding of poplars was undertaken in 1924 in the United States.[3] But the real breeding of forest trees was started in the United States by a lumberman.

In 1925, Mr. James G. Eddy, owner of a large timber tract in the Pacific Northwest, founded a tree-breeding station in the Sierra Nevada of California. The selected site was at an elevation of about 2000 feet, just above and overlooking the town of Placerville. Mr. Eddy decided to breed the most valuable species for forest industries. He selected pines.

The place chosen for the Eddy Tree Breeding Station was ideal. It was located amidst the second growth of ponderosa pines which had sprung up naturally after the virgin forest had been cut about a century ago. Some young ponderosa pines were already cleared to give room for irrigated pear orchards. The countryside looked like the northern foothills of the Alps in

3. For details see Ernest J. Schreiner, "Poplars Can Be Bred to Order," *U.S. Department of Agriculture Yearbook, 1959,* pp. 153–57.

Switzerland. Climate was mild, suitable for growing almost all pines of the world except a few tropical species. Water for nurseries was easily available when needed during the sunny, dry summer.

The whole Sierra Nevada with its various pines was like a big outdoor laboratory for studying the genetics of pines and developing methods for their breeding. On the low foothills of the California ranges grew Digger pine and knobcone pine. Above the breeding station were immense intact forests of ponderosa pine and Jeffrey pine with a generous admixture of sugar pine, which was replaced higher up by its handsome first cousin, western white pine. Above the ponderosa-Jeffrey forests was a large belt of lodgepole pine and, in the alpine habitats, grew whitebark pine and limber pine. Farther east and south was bristlecone pine. Across the valleys—the Sacramento valley to the north of San Francisco and the San Joaquin valley to the south—were still more pines in the coast ranges. All told, there were nineteen species, more than anywhere else in the world except Mexico, and even Mexico with its diversity of species was not too far to be included in the pine-breeding program.

With the founding of the Eddy Tree Breeding Station, the science of forest genetics was born. Foreign pines were planted at the station in a large pine arboretum, to be crossed with native American pines. Soon after its initiation, tree breeding revealed undreamed-of possibilities for the improvement of pines. It was an entirely new endeavor for foresters. Careful notes had to be kept of the time pollen was released from different pines, of the time the little female conelets were mature enough to accept pollen grains. (If one week is missed, a whole year's work is lost.) Implements had to be invented to protect the conelets from contamination by undesirable pollen.

Pollen had to be collected from the branches of tall pines and tested in the laboratory. The artificial pollination of conelets high in the tree crown was as complicated as the fertility rituals involving pines in ancient times. A tree breeder, sitting one hundred feet above the ground on the branch of a pine, wearing a crash-helmet, and holding a hypodermic syringe full of pollen in his hand, was an amusing sight for many an old-fashioned forest worker.

After the conelets were pollinated, they had to be protected from squirrels, jays, or nutcrackers. At the end of the second summer after pollination, when the cones matured, ripe seeds would be extracted, cleaned, and kept in cold storage to preserve their viability.

When pine seeds were planted they did not always germinate so promptly and abundantly as do vegetables. This resistance to germination is common in wild plants; it is their ecological defense against the adversities of the environment such as early summer drought or late frost. In domesticated plants, resistance to germination has been bred out by thousands of years of coddling and selection. It was not so with forest tree seeds. Ways had to be found to force the stubborn seeds of some pines to germinate well and all at once, when needed. Seeds had to be planted in moist soil and chilled but not frozen for a couple of months or more in a refrigerator.

Artificial chilling was nothing else but an imitation of the natural ecology of pines. Seeds of Scots pine from Siberia, where cold winter changes rapidly into warm summer with practically no spring in between, needed no chilling. On the other hand, seeds of Digger pine will not germinate without chilling. Digger pine, which grows in the California foothills where winter is mild and temperatures fluctuate between 30° F and 50° F requires a prolonged chilling of its seed. Because there are so many variations in the chilling requirements of pine seeds, the reader is advised to consult a seed manual.

The busiest part of the year at the Eddy Tree Breeding Station was the time when seeds were sown in nursery beds. All hands took part in the sowing; it was like an ancient annual spring festival celebrating the return to life of the slumbering world. When seeds germinated, slender seedlings were counted, measured, and any signs of superiority were carefully recorded. The following spring, the promising ones were promoted to transplant beds for a year or two and then outplanted in the woods. There the little pines would be on their own but still watched carefully by the breeder.

When the tree breeding station demonstrated the possibilities of applying genetics to forestry, Mr. Eddy donated it—lock, stock, and arboretum—to the U.S. Forest Service. The station was renamed the Institute of Forest Genetics, and its arboretum became known as the Eddy Arboretum.

F. I. Righter, who joined the Institute in 1933 as the first geneticist on the staff, invented the new methodology needed for pine breeding, and his techniques, with only a few modifications, are used throughout the world today. As work at the Institute expanded, Righter reported that pines can be crossed to a much greater extent than had been thought possible, and that pine hybrids were fertile, often displaying "hybrid vigor."[4]

It was also found that the two large subdivisions of the *Genus Pinus*—haploxylon, called white or soft pines; and diploxylon, known as yellow or hard pines—possess definite genetic barriers preventing their intercrossing. Within the two subdivisions, some species had strong genetic barriers; others, considered by some botanists as valid species, did not possess such barriers. This discovery invalidated for pines the opinion of some botanists that "good," that is, easily identifiable and valid, species do not cross with other "good" species.[5]

Many pine species were tested at the Institute for their hybridizing capacity. No general pattern emerged from the behavior of pines. Every species had to be tested repeatedly. Italian stone pine, which does not hybridize in nature, also could not be forced to cross in captivity. Torrey pine would cross only with Digger pine and completely rejected all other pines.

Occasionally, cases behaved in a puzzling manner. Bishop pine (*Pinus muricata*), occurring in a string of several little groves along the Mendocino coast of California, refused to cross with all other pines of the same group. Moreover, northern populations of this pine do not cross with its own southern populations. Each grove behaves as an independent species. "The

---

4. F. I. Righter, "Evidence of Hybrid Vigor in Forest Trees," in Theodore T. Kozlowski (ed.), *Tree Growth* (New York: The Ronald Press, 1962), pp. 345–54.

5. This opinion apparently was based on the dictum of the French naturalist of the eighteenth century, Georges Louis Buffon, who said that different animals usually do not hybridize, and, if they occasionally do, as in the cross between jackass and horse, the hybrid is always sterile. Later, Buffon's ideas were extended to plants, and his concept of genetic infallibility of species is still shared by some scientific writers. About "good" and "bad" pine species, see N. T. Mirov, *The Genus Pinus* (New York: The Ronald Press, 1967), p. 531.

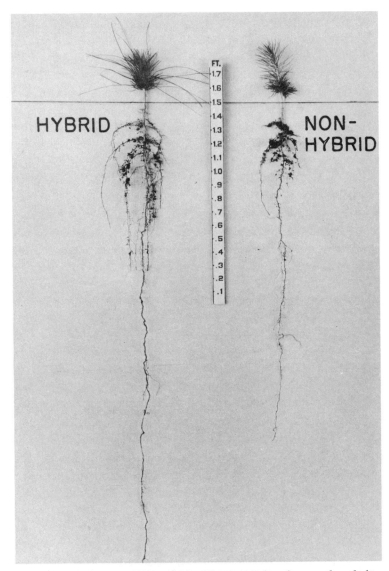

Left: A ponderosa pine crossed with an apache pine produced the sturdy, well-rooted hybrid seedling. *Right:* A nonhybrid ponderosa seedling. Both are from the same seed-tree and are one year old. Note the precocious appearance of long secondary leaves on the hybrid; the nonhybrid will have them in its second summer. The ragged appearance of the root systems just below the stems of both seedlings is caused by mycorrhizal growth. (*U.S. Forest Service Photo*)

closest parallels to the situation in Bishop pine appear to be the sibling species—morphologically similar but reproductively isolated populations—which are common in some groups of animals and plants."[6]

The genetic affinity of pines growing on both sides of the Pacific demonstrated their amazing stability. These pines, separated for many millions of years, have retained not only the same number of chromosomes but also their structure and their physiology. When brought together, they behave as though they had never been separated; some unite voluntarily, others need the help of tree breeders, but only a few pines have changed so much that they have lost their ability to interbreed with other pines entirely.

Inability to hybridize was caused either by the nature of the pine or by inadequate technique. By learning more about the inner mechanisms of the stubborn pines and by improving the technique of pollination, tree breeders overcame resistance to hybridizing in many pines. The most spectacular case of resistance to pine hybridization was shown by California's royal sugar pine, the undisputed queen of all pines. She is a white pine, but she never would cross with other white pines, either in the wilderness or in the intimacy of botanical gardens. Tree breeders at the Institute tried to help her, but she refused to condescend from her aloof isolation. Only after several years of repeated attempts by tree breeders did sugar pine accept another pine's pollen, and it was not of any American white pine but of two Asiatics—Chinese *Pinus armandii* and Korean *Pinus koraiensis*. Alas! The hybrids were not so tall as their mother but perhaps were more vigorous.

Other American white pines were not so choosey. Eastern white pine was crossed with Himalayan white pine, and western white pine with Macedonian white pine. Mexican white pine and Himalayan white pine did not even need assistance from tree breeders. When planted in an English arboretum, they soon intercrossed. The baby was named *Pinus holfordiana*, after Sir George Holford.

The ease of interbreeding white pines of America and Asia

6. W. B. Critchfield, "Crossability of the Closed-Cone Pines," *Silvae Genetica* 16 (1967):89.

Swiss stone pine (*Pinus cembra*) at an elevation of 6400 feet in the southeastern part of Austria (Steiermark). In its alpine habitat this pine has a remarkable capacity to maintain a timber form with tall, straight trunk. (*Austrian Forest Research Institute.*)

was of utmost significance. It showed that they originated in the same place, and that that place was in the extreme North, where two continents once were connected.

Hybridization among hard pines was suspected a long time ago; it puzzled herbalists, and, apparently, caused Linnaeus to limit, in his *Species Plantarum* (1753), the number of pines to five: three European (Swiss *Pinus cembra*, Italian *Pinus pinea*, and *Pinus sylvestris*) and two American (eastern white pine and loblolly pine). Linnaeus evidently thought these were "good species," that is, they did not hybridize with other pines. He omitted other European pines which had no clear-cut genetic barriers. Later it was found that three of the five Linnean pine species do hybridize with other pines. They are Scots pine (*Pinus sylvestris*), American white pine (*Pinus strobus*), and loblolly pine (*Pinus taeda*). All cross readily within their group. Apparently no one yet has crossed Swiss stone pine successfully, and the natural hybrid between loblolly and longleaf pine is *Pinus sondereggii*, known to foresters as "bastard pine." Obviously loblolly did not behave as a good Linnean species should. Also there is no doubt that *Pinus cembra* would cross with *Pinus siberica*. They are very close to one another and some botanists even consider them to be the same species. Of the five pines, only Italian stone pine still maintains its reputation as a good Linnean species. It does not cross with any other pines.

Botanists encountered much confusion when they attempted to classify the hard pines of Mexico, where the pines intercross so freely that it is often impossible to say where one species ends and another begins. Breeding Mexican pines at the Institute of Forest Genetics was limited to only a few species, of which a cross of ponderosa with Montezuma pine was successful. The enormously rich breeding reservoir of Mexican pines still awaits exploration.

Inevitably there were disappointments in the Institute's work. All efforts to double the chromosome number in pines were futile. In herbaceous plants, doubling chromosomes was not uncommon and often resulted in bigger and better tetraploids and polyploids. But pines turned out to be the most resistant in this respect. They guarded well the ancestral integrity of their twenty-four chromosomes. When exposed to chemicals like colchicine or to x-rays, heat, and what-not, they would either become malformed and die or recover and continue to grow normally with their natural number of chromosomes. Never would they become polyploids!

The Institute of Forest Genetics became a Mecca for foresters and tree breeders from all over the world. Many young men from different countries learned at the Institute the intricacies of breeding forest trees. Gradually tree breeding stations were established in Canada, Mexico, all European and Asiatic countries, and in the lands of the southern hemisphere. There are now two more forest genetics federal establishments in the United States, one in cold and snowy Wisconsin and the other in warm and humid Mississippi. Big lumber companies in the United States also employ forest tree breeders.

The old way of selecting the best looking pines in a wild forest is still used, but it is done now with complete understanding of the laws of genetics. Superior pines, called "plus" trees, are selected in the woods. Their branchlets are clipped off and grafted onto any suitable rootstock of pine, either planted earlier in "seed orchards" or grown in pots, later to be outplanted to form an orchard. Because the cuttings are a part of mature seed- and pollen-bearing trees, they are capable of producing pollen and of bearing seed soon after they are grafted and moved to the seed orchard.

Seed orchards are usually located not too close to the wild woods of the same pine species, lest stray wild pollen pollute the orchard. The pines growing in a seed orchard are like children selected for their high IQ's and put into a special school. The children exchange ideas with their peers, freely and fruitfully; the selected pines exchange their superior pollen with other grafted pines of the same orchard.

To be safe, the seeds gathered from the orchard pines are planted in nursery beds, and the seedlings are tested again. If their quality is up to expectations, the seeds in the orchard are harvested and distributed among happy lumbermen. The final result is a superior pine forest.

Pine seed orchards can be found in many countries: in those of northern Europe, and in New Zealand, Australia, Canada, and the United States. The southern United States is especially

When mass production of pines from superior trees is desirable, foresters often use vegetative propagation. Illustrated here is a successful experiment in this technique conducted in 1942. *Above left:* A 6-inch Monterey pine cutting, or slip, has developed abundant roots after planting in moist soil. *Above right:* Six years later, N. T. Mirov stands beside the transplanted cutting, now a healthy symmetrical tree, 5½ feet tall.

Left: The same tree 20 years later, more than 32 feet tall. In 1975 it is still growing well at the Institute of Forest Genetics, Placerville, California.

suitable for creating man-made forests, because pines grow fast there. Some southern pines, mostly slash and loblolly, also are doing well in the lowland orchards of Argentina and Brazil. Monterey pine is an excellent species for seed orcharding in New Zealand and Australia; its growth is phenomenal and it is the easiest pine to propagate vegetatively.[7] Seed orchards also are used for growing pine hybrids. The procedure, of course, is much more complicated.

Replacement of wild pine forests with domesticated trees is a slow process, but foresters are trained in caring for their long-lived charges. Often a pine breeder will not follow his hybrid to maturity; others who succeed him will. His work is based on faith in the future. But when he is lucky enough to see his babies grown up, matured, and harvested, to be replaced again with superior trees, he is the proudest and happiest man in the world.

Toward the end of this century we will see, in the warmer parts of the world, extensive planted forests of man-made pines; in the cooler regions, the progress will be slower. Gradually all productive pine forests will be replaced with genetically improved trees of rapid growth, longer fibers, heavier wood, greater resistance to insects and disease—trees containing more cellulose and less lignin.

Efforts to improve pines also will be concerned with developing and enhancing their natural beauty. Much has been done with the ornamental use of pines in China, Japan, and the Mediterranean countries. The landscaping of a Japanese temple calls for trimmed pines (*Pinus densiflora* and *Pinus thunbergiana*). An Italian landscape demands the "umbrella pine" (*Pinus pinea*); Via Appia would look naked without it. These pines are well domesticated.

Often wild native pines also are used in landscape architecture. *Pinus pseudostrobus* of southern Mexico and Central America, an extremely handsome tropical pine, is planted much in the

7. Vegetative propagation of Monterey pine was first reported in 1934 by a New Zealand forest ranger, in a little known forestry magazine with a Maori name, *Te Kura Ngahere* 3:185. In the United States, early work on rooting and grafting pines for forestry needs was done first at the Institute of Forest Genetics in the 1940s. See N. T. Mirov, "Tested Methods of Grafting Pines," *Journal of Forestry* 38 (1940):768–77 and "Experiments in Rooting Pines in California," *Journal of Forestry* 44 (1942): 199–204.

Slash pine, one of the most beautiful pines, is also one of the most important pines of the American Southeast. (*U.S. Forest Service Photo*)

gardens of Guatemala; Mexican *Pinus patula* is planted more and more in the landscaping of California homes, and the Canary Island pine is a favorite species when a stately effect is desired. A dwarf variety of European Mugo pine (*Pinus montana*) is a handsome potted ornamental for patios.

Scots pine, a favorite conifer for planting in the prairies of the United States and Canada, is becoming also a popular Christmas tree. And there are Japanese Bonsai dwarfed pines, which demonstrate that one may enjoy the beauty of pines even when a garden is limited to the window sill of one's apartment. Any pine can be grown as a potted plant.

Mexico is especially rich in various pines that can be included in the list of ornamental trees—different varieties of Montezuma pine, and the stately Durango pine which has six, seven, or even eight long needles to a cluster instead of the two, three, and five of most pines. More needles make the crown of the Durango pine more delicate and handsomely fluffy. There is also Lumholtz pine, whose foliage looks like a horse's mane; or Pince's pine, which resembles a weeping willow tree more than a pine. The ornamental values of pinyon pines, both of Mexico and of the American West, are yet little explored. Other Mexican pines have all the prerequisites for becoming garden trees except, perhaps, for their frost tenderness. For example, the craggy Chihuahua pine, a species that grows in the Mexican state of Chihuahua and extends to southwestern New Mexico and southeastern Arizona, is an attractive ornamental whose name makes it a good conversation piece. Some day frost tenderness may be bred out of some pines by crossing them with cold-hardy pines.

But that is not all. In breeding pines for good lumber or long fibers, the tree breeder occasionally finds among his seedlings some mutants that a forester would discard. They are useless as commercial trees, but they might be invaluable for ornamental and landscape plantings. Don't destroy freak seedlings. It is possible that, sometime, the main purpose of some pine-breeding projects will be to develop pines not for their commercial qualities but for their aesthetic values.

In the future, even commercial pine forests will be as beautiful as virgin forests. Only a trained forester will be able to see

This 47-year-old Monterey pine forest in Canterbury Conservancy, South Island, New Zealand, is an example of a planted forest that doesn't look planted. Monterey pine is unique among pines because, although its native habitat is an extremely small area of California, it has through plantings expanded into millions of acres in the southern hemisphere. (*New Zealand Forest Service*)

that they are planted. They will be used as wild woods for rec-reation. People will stroll through the man-made forests as they strolled through virgin pine woods; or they will sit around camp-fires enjoying fragrant pine smoke that rises up to the stars. They will sing the songs their forebears sang before them in the wilderness of uncut forests.

Someday, old overmature pines, majestic in their splendor and decay, will be found only in sanctuaries, parks, wilderness reserves, and around Buddhist temples. Some of them will be known as progenitors of useful contemporary species. And there will develop in the wilderness (if any wilderness exists in the future) new pines, but that will take a long, long time. Pines lived on earth for many millions of years before man came into existence, and most likely they will be living for a long time after man disappears.

LIST OF PINE SPECIES AND COMMON ENGLISH NAMES

WHAT'S IN A NAME? That which we call a pine would smell as sweet without any name, but we do need names for the study of pines, and the good rules of botany require that each pine species shall have a name in Latin, the international language of science.

We have mentioned that the important business of pine study was first recorded in ancient Greece when Theophrastus described several kinds. The name *pinus* has been in use since early Roman days when it was a common name. In medieval times *pinus* was the name of a group of trees having cones, sometimes including alders and birches. Early observers were not sure of the botanical place of pines until, in the seventeenth century, the French botanist Tournefort pronounced in a Latin treatise that *"Pinus est plantae genus,"* that is, the group of trees known among plants as *pinus* is a genus. Thus *pinus* became a botanical name. However, identification within the genus remained in a state of confusion until the early eighteenth century when Linnaeus brought order with his classification system (see footnote, p. 81).

The Latin names of pines may be descriptive, the names of localities, or the names of men who described them scientifically. When the people of various nations, provinces, and localities retain their own names for pines, scientists recognize these and record them along with the Latin names. Good examples of common English-American names are jack pine (*P. banksiana*), red pine (*P. resinosa*), and loblolly (*P. taeda*). The common names of white-bark and limber pines are simply translations of the Latin *P. albicaulis* and *P. flexilis*.

Following is a list of the botanical and common English-American names of pines and the general areas where they grow. It cannot be called a complete and final list because some forest areas—Mexico above all—have not been thoroughly explored. Even the familiar pines are not unalterably classified; new identification methods may lead to discoveries about pine relationships. However, this is a good working list for the present.

(PINUS)

albicaulis (western U.S.)	whitebark
aristata (Colorado)	Colorado bristlecone
arizonica (Arizona; Mexico)	Arizona
armandii (China)	Armand
attenuata (California; Oregon)	knobcone
ayacahuite (Mexico; Central America)	Mexican white
balfouriana (California)	foxtail
banksiana (northern U.S.; Canada)	jack
brutia (Mediterranean)	Calabrian
bungeana (China)	lacebark
canariensis (Canary Islands)	Canary Island
caribaea (Caribbean)	Caribbean
cembra (Europe)	Swiss stone
cembroides (Mexico)	Mexican pinyon
chiapensis (southern Mexico; Central America)	Chiapas white
chihuahuana (Mexico)	Chihuahua
clausa (eastern U.S.)	sand
contorta (western U.S.)	lodgepole
cooperi (Mexico)	Cooper
coulteri (California)	Coulter
cubensis (Cuba)	Cuban
culminicola (Mexico)	Potosi pinyon
dalatensis (Vietnam)	Da Lat
densiflora (Japan)	Japanese red
douglasiana (southern U.S.; Mexico)	Douglas
durangensis (Mexico)	Durango
echinata (southeastern U.S.)	shortleaf
edulis (western U.S.)	Colorado pinyon
eldarica (Trans-Caucasus)	Eldar (desert)
engelmannii (Mexico)	Engelmann
excelsa (Himalayas)	Himalayan white
flexilis (western U.S.)	limber
funebris (eastern China)	(no English name)
gerardiana (western Himalayas)	chilghoza
glabra (southeastern U.S.)	spruce
greggii (Mexico)	Gregg
griffithii (Himalayas)	(same as *P. excelsa*)
halepensis (Mediterranean)	Aleppo
hartwegii (Mexico; Central America)	Hartweg

heldreichii (Mediterranean) — Heldreich
hwangshanensis (China) — (no English name)
insularis (Philippines) — Luzon, or Benguet
jeffreyi (California) — Jeffrey
khasya (southeastern Asia) — Khasi
koraiensis (Korea, etc.) — Korean white
krempfii (southern Vietnam) — Krempf
lambertiana (California; Oregon) — sugar
lawsonii (Mexico) — Lawson
leiophylla (Mexico) — smooth-leaf
longaeva (western U.S.) — Great Basin bristlecone
longifolia (Himalayas) — (see *P. roxburghii*)
luchuensis (Ryukyu Islands) — Okinawa
lumholtzii (Mexico) — Lumholtz
massoniana (China) — Masson
maximartinezii (Mexico) — Martinez pinyon
merkusii (southeastern Asia) — Merkus
michoacana (Mexico) — Michoacan
monophylla (Nevada) — Nevada pinyon (in U.S.)

montana (Europe) — European mountain
montezumae (Mexico) — Montezuma
monticola (western U.S.) — western white, or Idaho
morrisonicola (Taiwan) — Taiwan white
mugo (Europe) — (shrubby var. of *P. montana*)

muricata (California) — Bishop
nelsonii (northeastern Mexico) — Nelson pinyon
nigra (Europe) — Austrian
occidentalis (Caribbean) — West Indian
oocarpa (Mexico; Central America) — (no English name)
palustris (southeastern U.S.) — longleaf
parviflora (Japan) — Japanese white
patula (Mexico) — drooping needle
peuce (Balkans) — Balkan or Macedonian white

pinaster (Europe) — maritime
pinceana (Mexico) — Pince's pinyon
pinea (Mediterranean) — Italian stone
pityusa (Mediterranean) — (no English name; we suggest Pity's)

ponderosa (western U.S.) — ponderosa

pringlei (Mexico)	Pringle
pseudostrobus (Mexico; Central America)	(no English name)
pumila (northeastern Asia)	(no English name)
pungens (eastern U.S.)	Table-mountain
quadrifolia (California)	fourleaf pinyon
radiata (California)	Monterey (radiata in New Zealand)
reflexa (western U.S.; Mexico)	(same as *P. strobiformis*)
resinosa (northeastern U.S.)	red
rigida (western U.S.)	pitch
roxburghii (India)	chir
rudis (Mexico)	(no English name)
sabiniana (California)	Digger
serotina (southeastern U.S.)	pond
sibirica (northern Eurasia)	Siberian stone (white)
strobiformis (western U.S.)	southwestern white
strobus (eastern U.S.)	eastern white
sylvestris (Eurasia)	Scots or Scotch
taeda (southeastern U.S.)	loblolly
taiwanensis (Taiwan)	Taiwan red
teocote (Mexico; Central America)	(no English name)
thunbergiana (Japan)	Japanese black
torreana (California)	Torrey
tropicalis (Cuba)	tropical
virginiana (eastern U.S.)	Virginia
wallichiana (Himalayas)	(same as *P. excelsa*)
washoensis (California; Nevada)	Washoe
yunnanensis (southeastern China)	Yunnan

There are no books in which all aspects of the whole genus *Pinus* are included, but *The Genus Pinus* by N. T. Mirov (Illustrated. 600 pages. New York: The Ronald Press, 1967) discusses paleobotany, history, geography, genetics, physiology, development (briefly), ecology, chemistry, and taxonomic problems. The book is very general, but one may find in it references to the original works that are scattered in many magazines and symposia, and in many languages.

Several valuable works have appeared in the field of taxonomy and distribution of pines. The most up-to-date information is in *Geographic Distribution of the Pines of the World* by William B. Critchfield and Elbert L. Little, Jr. (U.S. Department of Agriculture, Forest Service Miscellaneous Publication 991, 1966) and *Subdivisions of the Genus Pinus* by Elbert L. Little, Jr., and William B. Critchfield (U.S. Department of Agriculture, Forest Service Miscellaneous Publication 1144, 1969). These may be obtained for a small fee from the Superintendent of Documents, U.S. Government Printing Office, Washington, D. C.

Extensive information on pine seeds (and all other kinds of forest seeds) can be found in *Seeds of Woody Plants in the United States* (Illustrated. 883 pages. Forest Service, U.S. Department of Agriculture, Agriculture Handbook No. 450, 1974).

To the reader who would like to learn more about the morphological and taxonomic structure of pines we recommend a classic, *The Genus Pinus* by George Russel Shaw (Cambridge, Mass: Publications of the Arnold Arboretum No. 5, Riverside Press, 1914). The field has expanded greatly since 1914, but all the valuable fundamentals are there.

Many books have been published in the realm of ecology in

the last twenty-five years. We mention only two: *Plant and Environment* by R. F. Daubenmire (New York: Wiley, 1947) and *Concepts of Ecology* by Edward J. Kormondy (Illustrated. 209 pages. Englewood Cliffs, N.J.: Prentice-Hall, 1969). These two books give a good idea of the recent development of ecology, its present trend, and its application to forests. Kormondy's book is simply written and explains how ecosystems work; the only mention of pines is the description of one experiment with young planted Scots pine in England.

If a reader would become acquainted with the pines of Mexico, he should read the classical volume by the late, famous botanist Maximino Martinez, *Los Pinos Mexicanos* (In Spanish. 361 pages. Mexico City: Editones Botas, 1948). There is also *The Pines of Mexico and British Honduras* (In English. 244 pages. Pretoria: Union of South Africa Department of Agriculture and Forestry Bulletin No. 35, 1950).

INDEX